HIDDEN

TRUTHS, BROKEN SILENCE

CHRISTENE LEWIS

HIDDEN

TRUTHS, BROKEN SILENCE

A MEMOIR OF THE EVOLVING WOMAN THROUGH STRUGGLES

CHRISTENE LEWIS

First and foremost, to my loving children, Akil, Michael, and Ava, who have helped me to rise before my blinded eyes.

Raph, this is for you.

To my probation officer, Jamila Williams, and the City of Toronto staff, especially Stephen Linton (Big Bro).

To the staff, and especially my primary worker, Aisha "Renelle" John, at Rosalie Hall.

To my students at Agincourt Collegiate Institute, SATEC @ W.A. Porter Collegiate Institute, Monarch Park Collegiate Institute, and West Hill Collegiate Institute.

And to any young woman or man who is struggling to have a voice. I encourage you to trust in a positive adult who can help you build your path correctly. You, too, can make a difference. It only takes one voice, and it starts with yours.

The comeback is always REAL!

Kareem Bernard Lewis, our resting angel, I miss you. I love you. You were the realest one.

CONTENTS

INTRODUCTION 1

PAIN. 5

WHY. 9

DESPAIR. 13

MISSING. 17

WTF! 20

AWKWARD. 25

SYSTEM. 28

HELP. 31

TRICKY. 36

RIDER. 40

TOUCHY. 47

ALONE. 58

EMERALD. 64

LEAVE. 71

BROTHER. 76

BUILDING. 82

TIMING.	88
EXPLOITED.	94
DECISION.	98
UNIFICATION.	105
BLURRY.	112
NEW.	119
ADDITION.	128
LISTEN.	138
NO!	147
EYES.	154
HEAL.	162
DETERMINATION.	169
CHILDREN.	178
CHANGE.	186
LONGEVITY.	192

INTRODUCTION

Dear Uncle,

I've been trying to figure out how to come for you, because I'm legal now. Don't think I've forgotten the shit you did to me. You think I don't remember all those days and nights, but I know there's one day you won't forget. That Friday the 13th was the day you thought you took all of me. Yes, you were stabbed and beat up, but don't think I feel sorry for you. You always used my body to try and get your dick up. You molested me all the time, and I got tired of it, so I did what I should have done. I called up my boys, and they were there on a flip of a dime. While in the hospital bed, you were just concerned about going to jail, not even about the fact that you were in pain. You're lucky we live in a broken police system, because they believed your ass and gave you a pass. But you know the truth. You're living a lie, hurting little girls, especially me, but now I am older and I'm done crying in these sheets. Several charges were laid against me that night; I might as well have been the one holding the knife. A part of me wishes I was there to see your pain, but what would I have gained? I lost cousins that night; they don't talk to me now. I guess they're mad because of the way I handled things. However, of my cousins, the oldest knows the truth of what really happened.

I still see you at holiday parties, and it disgusts me. When I look at my aunt, I wonder why she never trusted me. I watch her sit on your lap in front of me—does she think I wanted you? You were the one on top of me. I was a child, only about ten years old, when you first started to grope me. Now, more than ten years after that night, I sit back and think to myself, *"What if I never got you stabbed, and did only what was right? You would have been the one in jail, hoping that somebody would post your bail."* My dad and brother stood by my side that night. Trust me, they came out, and you're lucky they are not the gangster type. You got me looking for love in all the wrong places. It's now time for you and me to switch places. I know that day really fucked with you. You don't even know who stabbed you; you're still playing "Guess Who." I know you barely leave your house, and you have panic attacks. I'm still hoping I'll get to see the day you die. I have two boys and a daughter now, and I am glad I get to show them a real man—a real man provides, and is not there to take his wife's money in strides. You're a predator and an abuser. Why did you choose me? I'm not a toy I'm a keeper. I have a husband now who vows to protect me. When I showed him who you were that day at the funeral, he looked at the casket and said, "Don't test me." A part of me wants to go back to the streets and deal with you, but God showed me different, and said it's time for me to let go of you. I'm going to leave you to Him; He knows how to deal with you better than I do. He, too, will have you on your knees.

I'm a woman now. I'm strong, Black, and proud. Don't think you could ever get away with the same shit now. I'm still thinking of suing you, but I keep questioning myself, "What would that really do?" It wouldn't take the hurt out of me, just money away from you. One day the truth will all rise to the surface; be prepared, not surprised. You didn't win at all, because, as I said, I'm proud and I'm tall. Thank you for making me stronger. I know I can hold on a little longer. When I take my medication for my nightmares and anxiety because of you, I get mad and scream, "Fuck you!" I'm not going to do that anymore, because I'm not a referee and I'm not trying to even the score. I'm done giving you all of me. I hope you get to read this book. I would love to get to see the look on your face when you do. Those who really know will now understand that all my pain streamed from you, and the actions that I took were not to hurt my family, but to protect myself from a child molester—you!

PAIN

I feel cold inside, but everyone keeps seeing that warm smile on my face. I can't keep faking my emotions. Can I really heal if I keep pretending to be strong all the time? I keep repeating to myself, "I deserve all the abundance of blessings and positivity in my life." Diary, I say that to myself all the time. I'm starting to believe that I say that to convince myself I deserve better. My heart is broken, and I feel so bitter inside that it scares me. I need help. Diary, can you please help me? I'm here writing to you, asking you questions as if you can answer me. This is fucking crazy! I feel crazy inside. You're my last hope. Do not let me down, please. Diary, I am begging you. Just keep my secrets a secret, and don't switch up on me, even when you feel disappointed in me. I've been silenced for years by fear, anger, disappointment, and trauma, but I can't be who I'm supposed to be if I keep pretending. It's time to finally state what it is, and finish my journey in life with dignity. No more secrets and, more importantly, no more protecting those who have taken my innocence away from me.

Why is it that negativity from another person

is what pushes us to do better, to make them swallow their words? I think that's the weirdest shit ever. And I am guilty of that myself. Diary, one of my uncles told me, and I quote, "The only thing that you're going to be able to do is lay on your back. I can even bet you five thousand dollars. Christene, I will give you five thousand dollars if you finish college." I replay that shit in my head all the time. I was standing in his garage during a family get-together for a holiday. I remember that it was chilly outside, and the moment he said that, I looked back at my dad's car, wishing I had my own car so I could just leave. I was sixteen when he said that. I didn't even respond to him. All I did was stand there in silence until someone came so I could go back into the house. I don't even remember who came into the garage. All I know is that it was a male voice. As soon as I saw the shadow of someone coming, I walked away. I gave one of those fake smiles, with my head down. While walking up the steps back inside the house—the steps were beige—everything and everyone was in slow motion, but the noise was still as loud as ever. It was my cousin who screamed, "Chrissy!" with a smile on his face and gave me a hug. He was the one family member whom I could relate to. Diary, you know those people who families refer to as "the black sheep"? Well, that was definitely him and me. I swear he could sense that I was unhappy and uncomfortable. He always heard me through my silence. I knew everyone was mad at me in the family for what I did, but not him. It was as though he already knew I was telling the truth.

When my dad, brother, and I left, I was looking out the back window and silently crying, while holding conversations with my brother. Eventually, I gave up with the talking and told them that my head hurt, so I was just going to close my eyes until we got home. While crying with my eyes closed, I was mapping out where we were and how far away we were from home. As much as I wanted my bed, I didn't want to get out of the car. I wanted the drive to last forever. All I kept thinking the entire time was, *"Is my life really worth this? Why don't I just kill myself?"* And I thought of ways to end my life. Everyone focused on what I did, instead of on why I did it. I guess protecting myself didn't matter. I began to hate my family and other families, especially Black ones. *Is this what we do? Turn a blind eye, sweep shit under the rug, and pretend nothing happened? I know this can't be life. This is fucked up!* Diary, can you just read while I write to you? I'll explain everything to you from the beginning, but please remember, no judgment. I don't even know where to start with everything, but one thing

I do know is the day I felt in my heart and body that something wasn't right. I just didn't know it was going to lead to all of this. It doesn't even matter how old I am now. When someone has really hurt you to the point where you feel less than a human being, you remember the pain as though it was yesterday, and even worse, you remember what happened. You can feel that fucking shit in your veins, running through you faster than when you get a shiver in your body.

WHY

Diary, one of my older brothers was like a dad to me, and still is to this day. He is the definition of a "rider." We even created a secret handshake with each other, and I still visualize doing it with him on my wedding day. For a very long time, I blamed him for my uncle, and he didn't even know it. It really wasn't his fault at all. Let me explain myself, and hopefully you'll understand. The only reason I blamed my brother for so long was because I would always have nightmares, and in my nightmares, I would always be screaming at him to help me, but he couldn't hear me. I felt as if I were screaming through the strongest piece of duct tape wrapped around my mouth. The first time it happened was in the summer. I would often spend weekends and parts of my summer vacations from school at my aunt and uncle's house. My brother had come to pick me up from their house. I remember him standing there at the front door. From where he was standing, he could see everything in the house, including the dining room, but we called it the play room, because that's where my cousins and I would usually hang out and play around with each other. I started to say goodbye to my family, gave them a hug, and said, "I love you." Diary, you know what I mean. Then I said, "Bye" to my uncle. He began play-fighting with me. I didn't feel anything was wrong until he got me on the floor. He was on top of me, and he put his full body weight on me and rotated his groin in a circular motion like someone trying to fix their watch on their wrist. I felt his penis firmly against my body, and I looked at him in discomfort. But when I looked at him, his face said something completely different. His face looked like he was enjoying what he was doing. His face went red, and he grunted with pleasure, "Yeah," while trying to play it off with laughing. That's when I first felt something was wrong. The entire time, my brother was standing at the door, laughing and talking to my cousins for a bit. I knew he thought it was just playful, but my heart, body, and soul knew different. I don't even remember how everything ended. I just remember glancing at my brother and thinking, *"Why are you not helping me?"*

Diary, I know I should have said something from then, but remember, I was one of the black sheep in my family, so who was really going to believe me? One thing I did know was that I did not want to go back there, especially if my feelings were right. *Was I overreacting to one situation? My uncle wouldn't hurt me, would he? No, I'm tripping. I'm thinking way ahead of myself.* Just because my biological mom's dad molested her for years didn't mean that the same thing was going to happen to me. And yet the next time I was at their house, I was quickly stricken with the feeling of truly being my mother's child.

We were sitting on the bottom steps of the staircase, because my uncle was leaving to go somewhere. He was talking to my cousins and me before we walked away. Well, at least my cousins walked away. He called me back for a second, and I said, "Yes, Uncle." He asked me to give his shoulders a massage, quickly.

I said, "For what?" And after a quick response from him, stating that it was just for a second, I began to place my hands on his shoulders. As I did, he reached behind his back and put his hand up my shirt and began rubbing and squeezing my breasts. I felt frozen inside. I was in shock, and I got really scared. I couldn't even say the word "stop." I genuinely didn't know what to do. I was around ten or eleven years old. He had no regard for what he was doing. When he was finished touching me, he just got up and left. I sat down on the stairs and waited to hear the garage door open, so I'd know he left. I felt stuck in time as I sat on the steps, but my heart stopped beating fast, knowing that he was gone. I went to the kitchen, picked up the phone, and called my dad. The moment he picked up the phone, I began crying, begging him to come pick me up. He asked why, but I couldn't tell him. I just cried and cried some more. Obviously, my dad never came for me. He probably just thought I was bored or something. Daddy, if you only knew. I just couldn't find the strength to tell him. I just went to the couch in the living room and watched TV with my great-grandmother. Diary, this shit continued for years—my uncle groping on my breasts and vagina. I felt as if I was his toy. I didn't know what to do, but I knew I was on the verge of snapping.

DESPAIR

There was one night when I fought back against him, hoping he would stop, but that didn't help at all. It was my cousin, him, and me in his and my aunt's bedroom. They had a computer in there. My uncle was sleeping; well, at least I thought he was. My little cousin was on the computer talking with friends online. My uncle rolled over on the bed and tapped my back. I was sitting on the edge of the bed, watching my cousin online. He was asking for another massage, and I said "no," but still ended up doing it. I don't remember what he said, I just remember my cousin defending him. The thought crossed my mind that he may have been molesting my cousin also. If he was, one thing I know is that I would kill him. She was the princess of the family. She was so smart. She's the only person I know that got more than one hundred percent on report cards, and could wait until the night before a big project was due to complete it, and still come home with a perfect mark on it. She and I would always talk about what we wanted to do when we got older. We both wanted to be doctors, but not an ER doctor. We wanted to be paediatricians.

We both loved kids. Anyways, to continue with that night, he reached down the top of my pants and began playing with my vagina. It was dark. The only light was from the computer screen. I guess it got too quiet, because my cousin looked over at him, and he slowly took his hand out. It didn't take long for him to try and put his hand back there. That was when I took his arm and stretched it to the back of his head. He said, "Okay, okay." He then pushed me, and I went right back to watching my cousin on the computer. I was hoping that, since I had fought back, he would stop. He left me alone for the rest of the night.

Diary, I wish you were there back then; I needed someone to vent to. I acted out in my early years, due to my parents separating and divorcing, but it only got worse in my teenage years. I completely blame my uncle for that. But I'll give you a break from hearing about my uncle. I know you must be tired of hearing about him. I feel as if it doesn't matter what I have to say to you; it's all negative. My life is filled with dark holes. I'm telling you, it's so much easier to just take my life, which I've tried doing more than once, but we will get to that later. Let me just talk about my parents for now. I'll briefly explain to you what I know about their divorce, and what I remember from the day my mom left. You might need a separate page to map out my family dynamics, so you don't get confused. Keep up, Diary.

So I mentioned having a biological mother, which might have left you with a lot of questions. My adopted dad is really my granduncle. My biological mother is his niece, which makes me his grandniece. My adopted parents had a child. He is my brother, but biologically, he is my cousin. My adopted parents remarried after getting divorced. I have more than one dad and mom. A lot of people would consider me blessed, and I do, too, but that's not how I've always felt. I was adopted from birth, or soon afterwards. I grew up with a family that wasn't my own, but at the same time was. When my mom left, I stayed with my dad and brother. At times, my brother was both my brother and my father. He would often save me when I would get in trouble with my dad. Diary, you could say he was my partner in crime, but in a good way. Every time he helped me to not get in trouble with my dad, you better believe he would be talking to me about changing my behaviour and improving, not just as his sister but also as a young woman. Whenever I heard him calling me from his room, "Christene, come here for a second. I need to talk to you," I knew I was about to get lectured. I knew he cared for me a lot, because he would often cry while talking to me. My dad, on the other hand, I hated when I was younger. I say "hated," because that's what I would often say when I was younger, not understanding the strength or true meaning of the word. Before I get into why I hated him, I want you to know that he is now my best friend, and we talk to each other every day, sometimes several times a day. He is what many people these days call a "rider" or refer to as "My A1 from day 1."

MISSING

⊰❀⊱

Diary, I remember the night my mom left; well, at least I think I do. I remember begging my mom not to leave. I remember my dad standing at the door while I stood at the top of the stairs, in confused silence, after she left. Diary, I don't know if this is real, but I remember this very clearly: My mom was at the door with her hand on the door knob, and I was weeping and saying, "Please, Mommy, don't go. Please." I remember attempting to jump on her back. The top stairs light was on, and there was a green carpet close to where the shoes were. The one thing that stood out to me was my mother's face. While I was crying, she gave my dad a look that I vividly remember. It was as if she was saying, "You're going to just stand there looking at me while our daughter is crying?" And his look in return was saying, "You deal with it. Nobody told you to leave. Her pain is on you." Diary, as I describe this to you, I honestly can't tell you if what I remember was a dream or if this really happened. All I know is that it still has an impact on me to this day. I obviously never understood what drove my mom to leave. I probably will never understand. And to be totally honest with you, Diary, I don't think I truly want to know, because I do not want to lose any respect for my parents. At the time, I blamed my mom for hurting my brother, my dad, and me. Yet could I really blame her if she was leaving for the better? Or was I just blaming her for leaving me, her daughter? I hated her. I say to myself all the time, *"Why leave me and my brother, but, more importantly, why me?"* If anything, leave my brother. He could stay with my dad, because he is a male. My mom should have taken me, because I am a female. Diary, all I knew was that my life was about to change, and I was not prepared for it at all. Diary, what does marriage really mean? My biggest confusion is why does "I do" bring two people together as one in marriage? I'm still trying to figure that shit out. Marriage should be about more than just "I do." I feel hurt inside. I don't feel loved or wanted. My mom, my own mother, walked out on me. Am I that bad that she couldn't stay? Fucking talk to me! Explain this shit to me. I am too young for this, man. My tears can't even save me, because I don't even know what they mean. I just know what I feel. Just because I feel something doesn't mean that's what it is, you get me?

I was in a lot of trouble. All of a sudden, I kept messing up. It seemed I couldn't get anything right anymore. My mom said since the day she left, she started getting phone calls that I was misbehaving in school. I was bullying people, and lying to everyone. I didn't trust anybody. Everyone thought it was okay to just throw shit at me, without a single fucking explanation, and then wonder why I started acting up. I finally got to meet my mom's boyfriend. I was about eight years old when I first met him. He was quiet, but I thought he was cool. He spoke to me and always asked me if I was hungry—and who was really going to say no to food? If my dad was around when my mom came to pick me up for a weekend with her new boyfriend, they would use humour when things got awkward. None of their jokes was funny, though, especially when the joke was finished and then there was that dead silence, where everyone was waiting for someone to talk first. Yeah, that stupid shit. I had to listen to that fake bullshit almost every other weekend, for years.

WTF

What in the ENTIRE FUCK, Diary? Didn't I just tell you that I am tired of people throwing shit at me, with no real explanation of what the fuck is actually going on? No, I seriously can't do this shit. Where the fuck did this bitch come from now? Who is she? Why is she here? And when is she leaving? I am sorry, Diary, here I am asking you, as if you know the fucking answer. I thought my mom had moved on quickly, but goddamn, so did my dad. I met his girlfriend, and I don't like her at all. She's not my mom. She needs to go away, and I mean go away right now. Do you know that she came into my room, sat next to me on the floor, and asked me if she could play my word search game with me? *Umm, no, you may not.* But I answered her "yes" anyways. I hope she doesn't think that she is my new mom. She's just taking up extra space, and I don't like how my dad is focused on her. Didn't he just let my mom leave, with no hesitation, just a straight face? What the fuck is really going on in this house?

Diary, I couldn't stand to be around my dad. My resentment started to grow more and more as the years passed by. I didn't know who to trust anymore, but I knew there was one person whom I could always count on through all the bullshit. My brother played both the role of a sibling and that of a father. He was the only one I could be real with. I felt abandoned by my dad, you know. It's as if he stopped paying attention to me as soon as he got his new girl. I can admit that I was jealous. I felt let me down and abandoned. Didn't he just watch my mom leave? Why was he with someone else so quickly? I want answers to those questions. Diary, here is the joke, though not really a joke: There was one question that I asked myself, over and over again—Why was I okay with my mom having someone else, but when it came to my dad having someone else, I couldn't handle it? Something just didn't make sense to me. If you know the answer to any of these questions, Diary, please feel free to chime in at anytime, because I am just rambling, and you don't have shit to say, do you?

Things just seemed to be getting worse for me in every area of my life—from my emotions to my mental health. Even my physical appearance started to change. I started lying more, stealing, hiding things, and sneaking out. Diary, you name it, I probably did it. I knew my dad was getting sick and tired of my bullshit, but to be honest, I really didn't give a fuck. Every summer and every weekend, he would send me to my aunt's house. Don't get me wrong, I loved it there, because my cousins were there, and we were more like siblings than cousins. My excitement for going there didn't last too long, as I told you earlier when I first started to write to you, but I will let you know what happened. We would often go to visit my other aunts and cousins while I was at their house. We would go there regularly, and things would be alright, but there was one day that really messed with me, and to this day, nobody knows how much.

You remember I told you that I am adopted? Well, I've always known about that, but the way I met my biological mom was pretty fucked up, and the joke is that nobody else saw it that way. Couldn't they give a girl a heads-up before pulling stunts? Diary, let me tell you what these damn people did. It was one of those weekends when we were going to my other aunt's house in Scarborough. My cousins called me and told me to make sure I looked decent. I thought, *"What the fuck? I am going to wear track pants. It's just my aunt's house; it's nowhere special."* My cousins came with my uncle to pick me up from my dad's house, and we left to go over there. My uncle never stayed with us. He always just dropped us off, as if he were a taxi cab driver. Anyways, I am getting off topic, so when we got to my aunt's house, there were a few other people there. I didn't know two of them at all. Children are expected to have manners, especially in Caribbean households, so I said "Good afternoon" to everyone, or else I would get hit in front of everybody. I said "Hi" to the ones I didn't know, and I kept it moving. Do you know those times as a child when you want to go upstairs and hide away from everyone, but you can't leave the adults just yet, or else you'll be called rude? Well, that was me, just standing there, smiling and trying my best not to be awkward. While I was standing there, I noticed that one of people I didn't know kept watching me, and wouldn't stop. So I waited for my aunt to be alone in the kitchen, and I quickly ran in there. I asked her, "Who are those people, and why is that lady watching me so hard?" Are you ready for her blunt response, Diary? Because I wasn't. She said, "You know you're adopted, right?"

I said, "Duh, everyone knows," and I chuckled a bit.

"Christene, that's your mom sitting on the couch."

In my head, I was thinking, *"This is a fucking set up! I'm only fourteen years old, and you guys couldn't find any other way to tell me besides this way? Y'all are really fucked up."* Diary, before you lose your binding, and crumple all your pages in disbelief, I didn't say that out loud, but I wish I could have. I would have definitely earned myself some lashes across my back. I don't really remember how the conversation even started with her, but I ended up sitting next to her on the couch, and I called her "Mom." It felt weird to say, but I also didn't want to disrespect anyone. Also, my family is extra when it comes to that stuff. You could accidentally say something, and you'll hear them tell your entire family in Canada and back home in Jamaica that you tried to kill them.

AWKWARD

~ ⌘ ~

Diary, you may be laughing, but that's just how extra they can be. The only reason I called her "mom" was because she was my mom, and if I dared to call her by her first name, it would have been a big problem. It felt weird as shit, and wrong. I wondered if my dad and mom knew what was going on. And if they did know, why didn't they tell me? Who said I even cared to know who she was? The shit I heard about her from my family was nothing I wanted to involve myself with, especially as a teenager who already felt lost as fuck in this world. I really wanted to know why all of a sudden it mattered to involve this woman in my life. What did these people want from me? Diary, I told you, I already felt lost and confused as it is. I had a lot of shit going on, from my parents separating to their bringing new people into my life. I just couldn't process everything, and I wasn't trying to either.

After that day, it seemed as if everything just got worse. As I told you, my dad was tired of my behaviour, and I felt as if my family had set me up. Diary, you may not get how this can impact someone's life, especially when they are already going through a lot, but this situation messed me up. I didn't know how to trust anyone, or how to move around them. My dad was beyond fed up, and, for the first time, I could see that he was going through a rough time, but he wore it well. With a straight face and all. It was just the way he started moving. He didn't have as much patience as he did before, so if I said he was getting tired of my shit, then he was getting tired of my shit. My dad wasn't abusive to me at all. He wasn't one of those dads who came home from a bad day at work and took it out on their family, but when I got in trouble and passed my place, I would hear that belt jingling like Santa Clause's sleigh.

Diary, just so you understand, you're my confidant, so please don't fail me. I am telling you my truth. In a Caribbean household, physical discipline isn't abuse. It's used to set your child straight, especially when they forget the keyword, respect. I hated when I caught the belt from my dad. To this day, I can remember how that belt felt, and how I felt when I knew it was coming my way. I can laugh about it now, though. Have you ever had to do self-talk before a big presentation, because you're nervous? Well, that's what I had to do every time I heard that belt jingling down the hallway. All I kept thinking was, *"Don't cry, don't cry, don't cry, don't cry."*

I swear, each time, I tried to be more gangster in my attitude before I started feeling the hits. I was thinking in my head, *"You can't show him that this hurts. Be a soldier."* It was as if I was preparing myself for war. Diary, let me tell you how one day the opposing side of that war came through, and I can't lie, it was my fuck-up. This is why I told you, Diary, that you are the only one I trust completely, besides my brother. I was in high school, in the ninth grade, when I accidentally slipped up and said something to a friend. I told her what had happened the night before between my dad and me. But can you really blame me? That shit hurt like a motherfucker.

SYSTEM

A lot was about to change, and it was all over a cell phone. Can you believe that? A blasted cell phone. There's a reason parents don't buy that device for their children, unless they really need it. I borrowed my friend's cell phone for the weekend, and I hid the fact that I had the phone from my dad. Here's how events unfolded: My brother had come to pick me up from my aunt's house, and I ran to my friend's house, which was just two doors down, to give the phone back to her before going back inside my house. Man, my brother was so stupid that night. I thought he had caught my play, but clearly he hadn't. The man went inside and told my dad that I just went down the street. When I got back inside, I got the sweetest beating ever with a belt, and again, I said to myself, *"Don't cry, don't cry, don't cry, don't cry. Soldier style."* Diary, I told you the belt is cultural. It's normal to us, but others don't see it like that, especially different races. I just don't want you judging my dad. I don't want you to turn your back against me, too. Don't you think I sound crazy sometimes, Diary? You can't even talk back.

I went to school the next day—I attended Pope John Paul Catholic Secondary School, in Scarborough, Ontario—and I told my friend what happened and showed her the marks on my back. Have you ever played volleyball before, and you get the blood dots all over your arm from the bumping the ball so much? Well, that's what my back looked like. She went to my guidance counsellor and told her the whole thing. I was chilling in drama class during third period, when I was called down to the office. I had to tell them what happened and show them the marks on my skin. I had no idea what was about to happen next. That day turned out to be the longest school day of my life. Children's Aid Services were called, and they came to the school. I wasn't allowed to go home that day. The worker came out to the school to see me, and said she was going to get a police escort, so that I could go get my clothes, but none of that happened. Do you think I got one pair of jeans or socks or even a clean pair of underwear to wear the next day? And they wonder why people don't believe in the system, because they don't do what they say they're going to do. I found myself in foster care, and my dad found himself in a police station with child abuse charges. I was now convinced that my father hated me. And I mean, hated me from the depth of his soul. If he didn't hate me before, I thought he definitely hated me now.

The next day, I woke up in a house, to people I didn't know. Diary, of course, I got to meet the parents of the house before going to bed, but everybody else was sleeping by the time I got there. Like I said, it was one of the longest days of my life. When I woke up, I felt cold, but I guess I was so numb in my body and in shock because of what was going on that I just didn't care to really take in anybody in that moment. I wanted it to be a dream, but it wasn't. I wanted an escape, and I wanted it immediately. You know how some people say that they wish they could turn back the hands of time? Well, I sure as hell was one of those people that night and the next morning. My foster parents were okay, I guess. They seemed very nice and welcoming. They didn't ask me anything about my dad. All they wanted to do was make sure that I was comfortable. There were about four other children there. Two of them were teenagers, and the other two were actual children. I refused to eat breakfast there that day. I just wanted to leave and go to school. All that was on my mind was what I needed to do to not go back there. I had no intention of ever returning to that house. I felt like an orphan.

HELP

After school, I ran away to my aunt's house in the north end of Scarborough. I didn't want to be in foster care. I didn't know those people, and I didn't care for them. I was very uncomfortable, so I ran to my aunt. I knew she would listen. She loved to be in the mix, so I knew she already knew what had happened between my dad and me. I knew she would listen to what I had to say, because I had a lot to get off my chest. I'd been holding a lot of hurt inside for years, and since I bought you to finally tell you my story and how I really feel, I'll tell you that I felt little, smaller than an ant that could squeeze through the front door during the hot summer. Diary, I am going to tell you this from now, just because you know that you can run to someone and they will listen doesn't mean that they always listen to help you. Sometimes they listen just because they want to know what's going on, and to put their own twist to the story. I knew that I couldn't just run away and nothing happen. My foster parents called the police, so my aunt dropped me back "home." Diary, I just skipped a lot of parts about what I told my aunt when I ran to her house. I know I need to tell you, because I know I need to heal from it, so here I go. Remember what I just warned you about, okay Diary? When I ran away to her house, we had a long talk, and she was crying. She asked me why I was so aggressive and why I had such a bad attitude. Basically, she was trying to figure out what was wrong with me.

I looked up at her, with confidence in my eyes along with anger, and I said to her, "Maybe it's because my uncle is molesting me, and I can't tell anybody in this family, because I know they won't believe me." You want to catch the joke, Diary? She knew exactly who I was talking about, and asked me if I was going to tell my other aunt. I told her straight up that I didn't know what to do. I knew one thing, though; she wasn't going to help me. She wasn't going to help me at all. I know I gave you a break about my uncle, but I need to go back to him for a bit. My uncle had been molesting me from the time I was about ten or eleven years old. I may have been young, Diary, but I was still old enough to know when something wasn't right. Diary, I cry inside every time I fucking talk about this asshole. I still remember when it all started, like it was yesterday. I miss my family so much, and my cousins the most. I thought I could talk about him for a longer time, but I can't right now. Can we just go back to talking about my foster care situation for awhile?

I hated being there, Diary. I really did. I felt so alone. I didn't feel like that forever, though. I met a girl there, my foster sister, and we still keep in touch here and there, up to this day. I swear my high school life just went downhill after my being taken into foster care, but I was happy that I had someone to talk to now at home. Before that, I only had someone at school. I felt as if I became a product of the government. I felt like a slave in my own body. I had such low self-esteem, but I knew how to hide it well. I think I do still have it, to be honest. I am just trying to learn and grow through it. I still struggle with confronting myself as an adult. There's a lot of pain buried deep inside of me. I think I stayed in foster care for about a month, before getting out. My adopted mom finally came for me, because she said it was hard for her to watch me sit in foster care. I wasn't a part of the process of her getting me, but I could imagine it wasn't easy, because I now belonged to the government, not to her or my dad. The government doesn't make things easy for people at all. There's a meme on Facebook and Instagram that says something along the lines of, "I don't need to have sex, because the government fucks me every day." People may laugh when they read that, but they don't understand how much truth and depth there is to that quote.

She was successful in getting temporary guardianship of me. I went to go live with her and my stepdad in Guelph, Ontario. I got my own room. I would always tell my mom that I was going to put her in a retirement home when she was sixty, and then I would move into her house. I loved that house. My room had a balcony. I just loved it. However, I really missed Scarborough and my boyfriend at the time. I thought I would be with him forever. Diary, don't laugh at me. I pictured our children, buying our first house, and more. Ha-ha, I can laugh now. And before you even ask, no, I am not still with him, but he does pop up in my head from time to time, not because I still love him, but because I wonder what he is up to and what he has done with his life. One of my friends told me that she's seen him here and there on the road, and that he has kids now. We both just laugh about the love he and I had. We were young and dumb. Yes, he had other girls on the side that I found out about, but one thing he did was always protect me.

One day there was a situation where I was about to get into a fight with a girl at the bottom of a staircase at school. She made the first move and slapped me across the face, and just when I swung my arm to knock her the fuck down, this dude came out of nowhere and pulled me into the hallway and tried to calm me down, telling me shit like, "She isn't worth it." Who is really trying to hear that shit, when you want to fuck a bitch up? Yet he was right; she wasn't worth it at all, but I was so mad when he stopped me. He wrapped his arms around me and gave me a bear hug, and never let me go until I was calm. In high school, word travels fast. I was wondering, *"How the hell did he get here so fast?"* But I guess someone found out what was about to go down, and went and found him, and as the protector he was, he came and found me immediately. It was good while it lasted. I wish him all the best in life. Like I said, I missed Scarborough, and I began to display behaviours to prove it.

TRICKY

I took advantage of my mom, in a sense. I would refuse to do simple tasks, like go out with her and my stepdad. I would lie and steal, especially from him. I don't know why I did it. No, I am lying, Diary, I do know why. I thought he was rich. He was an author, and he had a really good job at some university, so what was a missing extra dollar really going to do to him? Again, Diary, that's what I thought back then, not right now. I just knew that I wanted money, even though I couldn't do anything with it, because I couldn't drive or anything. So what was I really doing with the money? I was so silly for that, and the good thing is that he has forgiven me for it, and for all the other dumb shit I did when I was staying there. While I was out there, I went to a Catholic school—St. James Catholic High School. I had to take the school bus for about thirty minutes each way to and from school, and on top of that, if I wasn't already feeling out of place—because Guelph is very different from Scarborough—I was one of only eight Black teenagers going there. I felt out of place, but that didn't stop me from making friends, joining a dance group, and being the lead in dance competitions. The friends that I made were pretty cool, but the lingo was very different from Scarborough, if you know what I mean.

I stayed with my mom for about six months, before returning to Toronto. I went back after the charges were dropped against my dad. I had to go to court and testify against him. I remember the fucking police officers asking me what I was going to say in court. I could tell they just wanted to win the case. They wanted to see my dad in jail. I couldn't even talk to my dad while I was in Guelph. When he would call my mom to check up on me, he couldn't even send a message through her to say "hi," or anything. One of the conditions was that he couldn't have any direct or indirect contact with me. I would yell, "Hi, Dad! I still love you," so he would hear me when he called. I was bad at my mom's house. I feel as if she didn't know me at all, even up to this day. There was one night in particular that I haven't forgotten. I remember yelling at my mom on the stairs, and my stepdad got involved, so I yelled at him, too. My mom said that that was her last straw with me. Since the charges got dropped, she shipped me right back to my dad, exactly where I wanted to be, in Scarborough. I was happy as fuck, but I wasn't happy about all the hell that broke loose when I came back.

Diary, I don't know where to start with all the madness that went down. I don't even know where to start with the bullshit. I went back to Pope John Paul Catholic School, where things just didn't seem to get any better. Diary, till this very day, I still think about whether I should have just stayed in Guelph with them, but at the same time, I don't regret anything that has happened thus far, because I wouldn't have been where I am today, or hold the values that I do. I started getting into fights at school, and one fight was really bad, in that it ended up on the internet. I could have been charged with aggravated assault, but thank God, the street code was in full effect back then. The girl I beat up was mutual friends with some of my friends, because we went to the same high school, and they said to her that if she snitched on me, they would ban her from the block. Diary, I know you know what a snitch is, so I'm not even going to bother to explain that to you. Just when I thought I was off the hook, guess what?

The school system was also in full effect, and I got suspended for that fight very quickly. I got in so much trouble with my dad. When I went back to school, everyone was "bigging" me up, thanking me for beating her up, because they didn't like her. I'm not even going to lie, I felt really good, and on top of the world, but that quickly came to an end when a rumour started that her friends wanted to jump me because of what I did to her. Apparently, people were calling her Harry Potter after the fight, because I had left a permanent scar on her forehead. So they wanted to do the same to me. Diary, you know that shit wasn't flying with me without a fight. I didn't give a fuck who they thought they were, I wasn't going down without a fight. I went home and prepared myself for the next day, just in case anything happened. I went inside my dad's toolbox in the basement and pulled out a hammer, and then I went into the kitchen and put a steak knife inside my Dora backpack. I told a couple of people that I had it on me, and that I was prepared for whatever those bitches had coming for me.

RIDER

I was amped. Have you ever gotten mad, Diary, and you get so hot that you can literally feel the blood running through your veins? Well, that was me. I felt like a ticking time bomb. Shortly afterwards, the school safety monitors came and brought me inside the office. Someone, and I say "someone" because I know exactly who it is, told them that I had a hammer and a knife in my bag. I refused to let the principal open my bag, but, eventually, he opened it. It seems as if everyone has to follow their policies and procedures, because he called the police. Diary, I say that so fucking sarcastically. The principal told me that he didn't want to call the police, because he really liked me. He always called me the diamond in the rough. I swear, it looked like he had tears in his eyes. One thing I remember him saying was that he was not going to leave the office when the police came. He told me he wouldn't put me in that position, because he knew I hated them. I wish I had listened to him, though. He told me that when they came, I should behave myself and not give them attitude. It was as though that advice went in one ear and out the other.

When they got there, Diary, you know I had already put on my don't-fuck-with-me attitude, but I quickly got put in my place. I swung to punch the officer in the face, and instantly they slammed me against the door and arrested me. I swear, I thought they were going to kill me. I know I am rambling, Diary, but everything just happened so fast. All I remember was my face slamming against the principal's office door, and the blinds that covered the window made a crumpling sound as if someone was trying to turn the blinds the right way. While I was walking out of the school, my boyfriend yelled, "Don't take my wife away!" And I won't even lie, I felt on top of the world, once again. I felt as if we were on some Bonnie and Clyde ride-together-forever type vibe, but he wasn't going to be sitting with me in that jail cell. I sat down in a cell for hours and hours, until a female cop—I swear, they think they're tougher than male cops—came in and spoke to me. I got released to my dad with conditions that included a promise to appear in court. I thought my dad was going to kill me for that, but he didn't. He never said a word to me that day, and to be honest, I don't think he and I really ever talked about it. Have you ever been so scared of your parents' silence when you know you fucked up, because you don't know what they are going to do to you? That was me. I was scared. I kept thinking to myself, "I am about to catch some hands, or some shit, but nothing came." Diary, his silence scared me even more.

My entire family knew what had happened, though. You see, Caribbean parents just love to chat. Before they come and talk to their child, they must first tell everyone back home in Jamaica, or wherever the rest of their family lives. Diary, I am still waiting for the belt till this day. But then it clicked to me that the reason why I never got the best beating of my life was because of my dad's charges. I know that, deep down in his soul, he probably wanted to beat my ass, but he couldn't. I got up in the system now, due to my ego and pride. So I started the court process, and went to the Scarborough courthouse at 1911 Eglinton Avenue. No word of a lie, I felt like a criminal, and they did a good job of making sure I felt like that. I was put on probation at the end of all that, and I thought that was that, but it sure as hell wasn't finished yet. My attitude just kept on getting worse. And the relationship between my dad and me didn't improve either. I started running away at night to go hang out with my friends, and that's when I met a guy whom I fell madly in love with. Well, at least I thought I did, Diary. Little did I know that he was one of the worst things that could have ever happened to me. I continued sneaking out late at night to go hang out with him and some of our other friends, smoking and drinking Olde 40's like it was water.

Time went on, and I became that ride-or-die chick for him, and for the block. I began beating up girls with one of my other friends, just because the guys didn't like them, or didn't want them in the area, or they were simply hoes in our eyes. We began stealing cars, and he would beat up any guy he thought was interested in, or looking at, me. Diary, there was one time when he stole a mini-bike from a guy. He did it slick, too. He rode it down the street and came back, then asked the owner if he could go farther, and then didn't return with it. The guy that he stole the bike from grabbed my arm and told me that if my man didn't come back with the bike, he wouldn't be letting go of me. So I told him that when he called his cell phone that he left with me to make it look as if he was coming back. Who the fuck told me to tell him what he said? Out of nowhere, because he had hung up the phone on me after I told him what was going on, he appeared with his friends and chased the guy around the entire area.

I just walked off as if I didn't know what was going on. I called everyone on the block, and we all came out and walked around the area like we were all couples, until we found him, while looking out for the police at the same time. Diary, when I said it was Bonnie and Clyde shit, I meant it. He tapped me on my shoulder, and I jumped. His shirt was covered in blood, and his knuckles were bleeding. I didn't even bother to ask him what happened. I just walked with him home and made sure he was safe.

Diary, have you ever heard the sayings, "What goes around comes around," and "karma is a bitch"? Well, karma came back to us the very next day. You see, he and his mom weren't close at all, because of his father, but I brought them back together. His mom lived far out West, and I would always travel there to go spend time with her, even if he wasn't there. She and I became friends. I would take pictures for her to send to her man that lived overseas. She would do the same thing for me. It was weird, but at that time, I thought it was cool as ever. One of our favourite things to do together was go to the store and buy frozen coffee drinks. We would go out to the store, whether it was cold or hot. The addiction to those drinks was real. I always felt as if she and I were really close, but I also felt it only took the slightest thing to get in between us.

He had a family member that had a lot of power over their perspective, and had a good way of putting things to his mother. The next day, my girl and his boy, along with he and I, stole two cars and got into an accident on the highway, close to Leslie and 401. All the glass was shattered in the car we had stolen. I had glass all over me, and I banged my head in the car. Our car got hit a couple times before coming to a stop. He and I ran off the highway, but I told him we should part ways, because he was on house arrest. I was willing to take the charge for him, because I didn't want him to get another charge on top of breaching his bail conditions. I pretended to have a seizure when the police came and had their guns pointed at me while I was running through the grass. I thought the police officer was going to shoot me. They took me to North York General Hospital, close to where we ran off the highway. I had a sprain in my neck, and was told to take it easy. The police called my dad to pick me up. My dad was upset, because I had told the doctor that I didn't want my dad to know any of my results from the testing that they did at the hospital. They have a policy in place that if you're sixteen and older, your doctor does not have to share your personal information with your family, if you don't want them to.

After all of my efforts to protect him and take the charges for him, guess what? The dumbass actually came to the hospital, just to see if I was okay. He ended up getting arrested in the process. Do you see and understand why I felt as if we were always on some dumbass, bootleg, Bonnie and Clyde stunt? I was released on another promise to appear in court, and he was remanded into custody. I cried every time he got arrested. I found out what jail he was in, and I called and pretended to be his sister, and they would let me talk to him, every single time. Ha-ha. Wouldn't you think they would do better with security? With him being in jail, there was nothing for me to do, so my dad saw that as a perfect opportunity to send me to my aunt and uncle's house, again. I told you, Diary, my attitude had gotten worse, so I didn't tolerate when people fucked with me. Diary, I am talking about that fucking disgusting uncle. When I went there, he was up to his same bullshit—touching me and grabbing my pussy. When I was washing my hands, this man stuck his hand down my pants, while my great-grandmother was sitting in the next fucking room. Diary, I got so tired of keeping it to myself.

TOUCHY

His molesting me started to consume me in so many ways. I wasn't even getting emotional about it; I was just getting more violent. I finally decided to tell my cousin what her dad was doing to me, and then she told me that she felt uncomfortable around another family member of ours. She then asked me if I was going to tell her mom, and then said that if I was going to do it, to make sure I tell her first so that she could leave the country. She was obviously joking when she said that last part, but she didn't want to be around when I said something. Let me tell you, my aunt was quiet and worked a lot, but when she was ready to snap, she snapped, and all everybody could do was be quiet, and say, "Yes, Auntie," and move out of her way, really fast. I felt better about finally getting it off my chest. At least my cousin knew now, and we spoke about the possibility of him molesting my younger cousin. We both said if we ever found out he had done that, we would both kill him. This shit is getting hard for me to write, Diary, because what I am about to write to you next still haunts me and fucks with me, to this day.

Diary, please bear with me as my tears roll down my face. You don't understand how it feels to be alone, especially when someone has taken your innocence, and you're constantly being thrown to him, because no one has a clue about what's going on. My boyfriend got out of jail, and I began seeing him as well as going back and forth from my abuser's house. It was a Friday in 2006, and I had finally had enough of his shit. I was living in fear. Not fear that he was going to kill me, but fear that he was going to touch me, and fear of the look on his face while he was enjoying it. It's a feeling that only someone who has gone through it, or is going through it right now, could understand. I had taken a shower and was walking out of the bathroom, and he just happened to be walking down the steps to leave the house. The moment he saw me walk out of the bathroom with my towel on, he turned back and molested me again. I locked myself in the bathroom until I heard the garage door open, so I knew he had left the house.

On that specific day, I felt helpless, because it was only me and another family member in the house, and they were downstairs watching television. Even though I would go there often, sometimes my cousins had their own thing to do, so they would leave and return later in the night. I then called my dad, crying, saying I wanted to go home, but I obviously didn't tell him why, and he wasn't having it. My dad would always ask me repeatedly, "Why do you want to leave there so badly, Christene?" And I wouldn't tell him anything. All I would say to him was that I just wanted to come home. I then called my boyfriend and told him what had happened, and then he told me to repeat exactly what I had just said. Then a friend, whom I referred to as my cousin, immediately asked for my location and wanted to ensure my safety. Diary, I felt like hell froze over that night. No, it was more like a stampede of wildebeests, but I felt like an ant trying to crawl out of the way before getting crushed.

I ran out of the house, with no shoes or jacket on, and that's when everything went down. One of the guys rang my uncle's doorbell. I knew my uncle would answer the door, and he sure did. One of the most meaningful people in my life was in the living room, and one of my older cousins, whom I had told everything, was upstairs on the computer. Diary, when my uncle opened the door, the guys beat him up, and he got stabbed multiple times, but the son of a bitch didn't die. I'm happy he didn't, to be honest. I wanted him to suffer. I ran away from the house to a stranger's house, and they called the police out of concern. I would've done the same thing. Imagine a teenager showing up at your door in the cold, with no shoes or jacket on. You better believe I'd call the police, too. They made sure I was okay until the police arrived. They also let me call my brother, so he came as well. The police arrived first. When my brother pulled up, they thought he was one of the guys that had stabbed my uncle, but then they quickly realized that my brother had nothing to do with my uncle getting stabbed, or why it happened. They had to verify with my uncle that my brother was not one of the people who had stabbed him. Diary, I thought my uncle would've said "yes," just to be a little bitch.

He came to the stranger's house that I had run away to just before the stabbing. When my brother saw me, he didn't even have to say anything. The look on his face said, "Why didn't you tell me?" The police took me to the station. It was right down the street, but boy, the car ride seemed to take forever. I was thinking about what to say and who to say it to. When I got to the police station, I got to see my older cousin, again. We both went inside an interview room. I said from the get-go that I didn't know who the guys were, but I also made sure the police knew that I didn't care about what had happened to him, and I explained why. Diary, I cried, I cried, I cried, and I cried some more. I even cried while yelling at my cousin, "I told you what your dad was doing to me!" And, Diary, they went quiet. Not even a mouse was quieter than they were at this point. At the time, I didn't understand why they didn't speak up. I was so mad at them, but I get it now. I hurt them, too. I should have told a responsible and caring adult, like my brother, dad, or mom, so that something could have been done about it appropriately. Apparently, my brother went to the hospital to see if my uncle was okay, out of respect for my aunt. Until recent years, I'd always thought that my dad and brother didn't believe me, I guess because the family was quiet about everything. They finally told me that when they went to the hospital, all my uncle was concerned about was what was going to happen to him because of what I said.

My brother and dad told me they knew that something wasn't right, and that things weren't adding up in the hospital, but just like everyone else, I knew they had to be in shock. Diary, I was the odd duck in my family, so I knew that this situation was not going to go over well, and that my word meant absolutely nothing to the majority of the family. All they did was talk more shit, and come up with their own version of what happened. I can't stand family. Diary, there is a big difference between family and relatives. I believe "relative" is just a word that binds people through blood and generations down the line. And "family" refers to those whom you commit to and who are committed to you as well. Family pushes you, as much as they can, for the better.

After we were finished with our interview, the police drove me back to my uncle's house, and my family was there. Before they drove me back, I could hear the two police officers laughing about the situation, while they smoked their Captain Blacks outside the police car. Diary, a Captain Black is like a cigarette. They have different flavours, like cherry and raspberry. Diary, I went off topic for a second, sorry. I still had no shoes or jacket on. While we were driving back, one of the police officers said they almost forgot what my uncle's house looked liked, because the police tape had been removed. My aunt looked at me and asked me if her family was safe for the night. I said, "Yes," because I insisted I didn't know who the guys were. I really wanted to curse every-fucking-body right there and then, especially one of my aunts. Diary, you remember when I was in foster care and ran away to my aunt's house? Well, that's the aunt that pissed me the fuck off that night. Remember, I told her everything about what my uncle was doing to me. That night, that bitch forgot everything. She was in my uncle and aunt's house with chocolate, giving it out to my cousins, and giving me a dirty look. In my head, I was thinking, *"Bitch, if you had said something, maybe this wouldn't have happened. But you have the nerve to stand there and try and judge me. Nah, fuck that."* Sorry, Diary, for the swearing. I just get so mad when it comes to this situation.

The police said that they would keep in contact with my dad to see if I would receive charges because of that night. Exactly eleven days later, we got a phone call from the police. They charged me with about thirteen offences in one shot. However, I didn't care about the charges, except for one. One of the charges said, "Falsely accuse person," which was there because they, and I say "they" as in the stupid police, charged me with that to protect my uncle. These police officers were beyond stupid, especially since they were white police officers dealing with a black family. They didn't give a fuck about black people, and certain regions were worse. Durham was the worst for me. They need some real training in common sense first, before anything. The police officers that I was dealing with for this situation didn't care what I said in the interview room. Did they even care to investigate? No, they didn't. At that point, I began to believe they were racist. I thought to myself, *"What if I were white? Would they have cared then?"* I was angry with the system, and to this day, I still am. It doesn't seem to be getting better; it seems to be getting worse, with all the racial profiling and circumstantial foolishness that happens between the police force and the Black community.

Diary, to put things into perspective, a Black man is the chief of police right now as I write this, but do you think anything is better? No. The racist ones definitely stepped up to the plate. They're not just mad at the Black community, but now they're also mad that their boss is Black, too. The police said that I falsely accused my uncle of molesting me. When I say I have a real hate for cops, it's real.

I wish we, as a whole family, could've sat down and watched my cousin and me in the interview room together. I was fucking livid! I went to a jail in Peterborough for about two weeks, before I received bail. I thought my dad wasn't going to come for me. When he bailed me out, I sat in the courtroom and cried in his arms for awhile. I remember him saying to me, with sadness in his voice, "I know you thought I wasn't coming for you." Diary, I may have been crying, but I was still angry. Have you ever heard of the honeymoon period, where things go well for a bit before shit hits the fan? Well, that's what happened. I was good for a little bit, when I first got out, but then I went right back to my old ways—not listening to my dad, sneaking out late at night, disrespecting his girlfriend, and more. My dad kept pulling my bail, and I would go right back to jail. To be honest, I didn't care what I did. The system had failed me, and I thought that my dad had failed me, too. Why didn't he say anything to my uncle? How come nobody said anything? I was angrier at my aunt that I had told when I ran away from foster care, and at my biological mother, because I had told her, too.

I'll never forget one of the times when my dad pulled my bail. Diary, I can laugh about it now, even with my dad, but it wasn't funny that night. I had snuck out to see my boyfriend that day and came back around nine or so, just before my curfew, according to my bail conditions. Neither my dad nor his girlfriend was home, only the basement tenant, whom I referred to as "Uncle" because he had lived there for so long. The house phone started ringing, and it was a private caller. I answered the first time, and the man on the phone asked if it was me. I hung up the phone and never answered again. My doorbell started ringing, non-stop. I crawled a kind of army crawl to the front window, and noticed two white guys standing at the top of the driveway. The phone calls kept coming, and wouldn't stop. So I then called the police and told them that there were strange men outside my house and private calls coming in. I don't know what told me to answer one particular call, but I did, and it sure as hell was a police officer stating, "If you do not come outside right now, we will kick down the door." I kept calling my dad, but there was no answer.

I turned off all the lights in my house, and I saw a blue light beaming through my brother's back window. These motherfuckers had my house surrounded. They made sure I couldn't run away. I knew I was going to jail then. I started putting on layers of clothes and taking strings out of my hoodies. The jail cells were cold and hard as fuck. I looked outside my window again before answering my door. My entire street was covered with police, just for me. I thought they were going to kill me that night. I opened the door, and, of course, a fucking female cop, all high and mighty, slammed me down on my stairs and arrested me with the rest of her crew. My stairs have metal edges, so that shit hurt. I didn't even fight or resist arrest, so her force was unnecessary. My uncle from downstairs came up, just to make sure I was okay, and began yelling at the cops, and they just pretended he didn't even exist.

When I walked outside my house, it was like the walk of shame. Every single neighbour was outside their house that night, looking at me being carried out in handcuffs.

There were at least fifteen police officers and several cop cars. There were cops from two different regions—Toronto and fuck-boy Durham—so I knew I had fucked up. The police then called my dad's cell phone, and he answered right away, and they let him know that they now had me. At that second, I knew my dad had set this up, and had pulled my bail. I hated my dad for that. To be honest, I still kind of do, but it's not hate, it's more like jealousy. I felt as if he'd chosen his girlfriend over me. I went back to Peterborough to jail. While I was there, it was an open-custody facility. I only spent one day there, before being transferred to a secure, locked-down facility in Kingston. The reason why they transferred me there was because the charges I had were serious, and I was one of the older girls there. They felt I posed a safety risk to the other girls in there. Diary, I am not even going to lie, I was scared to go to the Kingston facility.

ALONE

I called my dad there, and he would tell me every day that he might come to court the next day. My primary constable worker was a lady named Cheryl, but I called her "Cher Bear." She really took care of me, and I made it to a level called Distinction while I was in there. Diary, that means I was able to go outside more, stay up later, and go gardening in the shed. When you went to a secure jail, there were levels. There was the entry level, where you had an early bedtime and couldn't do anything. Then there was beginner, which meant you still couldn't do anything, but you were now used to the rules and had been following them. There was the advanced level, where you could stay up later, the staff trusted you more, and you had less cell time. However, before you made it to distinction, you would have to write a letter to the jail, explaining why you should be able to move up to that level. At distinction, you were able to get free time, and you could use the shed, where there were tools and shit. You became a leader, and would set the example for the rest of the women in there.

When I went outside, there was a big, tall, steel jail fence that closed us all in. There was another girl in there that was charged with second-degree murder, and I got really close with her. She and I began talking about what we wanted to do with our lives, and how we ended up there. There were some fucked-up individuals there. There was a girl who would blackout and start doing some crazy shit. She would pretend she was pushing out a baby, and even tried to attack a staff member one time. We all got locked in our cells while they dealt with her. One time she even took a piece of tissue paper and walked up to the wall, stating, "Make the blood go away. Go away, blood. It all needs to go away." I said to myself, "This bitch is fucking crazy, and I don't even want to know why the fuck she's up in here." She needed some real mental health help. I wondered what she did, but I was scared as fuck to know the answer.

When our cells locked, there was no coming out. If you needed to use the bathroom, you would have to knock until they heard you, and sometimes they took forever. Diary, my family did not come to visit me at all, and that pissed me off, but I only had myself to blame for that. They said there was no point driving two-and-a-half hours just for a thirty-minute visit, and then drive back another two-and-a-half hours. I watched a couple of the girls go in and out of that facility, while I was there. My dad continued to tell me that he would think about going to court each and every day, so I went to bail court each and every single day. I went to bail court forty-three times before I got out. I got sick and tired of being in jail. My lawyer was not happy with what I was about to do. I told him I'd do anything to get out. So I said, "Let's do a plea bargain." I plead guilty to falsely accusing a person and to public mischief, and the crown dropped the rest of the charges, because they knew that I wasn't the person who stabbed and beat up my uncle. It was hard to plead to the falsely-accuse-a-person charge, but I didn't care in that moment; I just wanted to get the fuck out of there.

I was tired of driving back and forth from Kingston to Oshawa, from Oshawa back to Kingston, and it finally clicked in my head that my dad wasn't coming to bail me out. He was going to make me learn the hard way. My lawyer was not happy about what I did at all, but at the end of the day, I got out, and that's all that mattered to me at that point. When I got out, I called my dad, and he was in disbelief that I was out. When he came for me, he spoke to a constable, and I felt as though he was asking questions to make sure that I would go back to jail if I didn't obey his house rules. Diary, can you believe that? I thought, *"Didn't you miss me at all?"* I was placed on probation for eighteen months, which would run consecutively to my other probation order for stealing the car. I told my probation officer everything, and I know I was hard to deal with, but one thing I always told her was that I was going to go to college and make something of myself. My probation officer never gave up on me at all, but my hatred for my father grew, and it grew, and it fucking grew some more. As the years went on, I started blaming him for my mom leaving, and for putting me in jail for a woman.

Diary, the next probation visit I had, I told my probation officer that I sat up on my bed that day, smiled, and said I wanted to kill my father. I swear, someone should really tell you, everywhere you go, to watch what you say, because your words are mighty and powerful. Guess what happened, Diary? I'll tell you what happened; I won't even give you a chance to think. Policies and fucking procedures. I didn't go home that night at all. My dad was called and asked to come in. The police were called, and I was voluntarily arrested. That means I agreed to go into the police car. If I didn't agree, then I would have gotten arrested under the Mental Health Act. I was arrested, but I wasn't charged or sent to jail.

Instead, I was sent to the hospital and placed on a form 1, on the psychiatric ward.

As if that wasn't scary enough for me, there was no room on the adolescent unit, so I was placed in the adult unit. My roommate was an old lady who drew pictures all day long. I swear to God, Diary, I thought she was going to kill me in my sleep, so I barely slept while I was stuck in that place. All I could think about was whether I was really crazy, and what I could do to get out of there. I felt as if my sanity was slowly slipping away each minute I was there. I was so scared, especially being placed with adults. Those people were grown. I was still a child. In my heart, I was screaming, *"Get me out of here, please!"* Before I was released, I had a whole team of doctors, nurses, and social workers around me at a table. The doctor told me that I wasn't crazy—thank God—but insisted I get mental health help, and added some additional conditions to my probation order. That's when I got connected to a central youth service downtown Toronto.

My worker was very cool. She even had the same name as me, Diary; she just spelt hers differently. She and my probation officer worked very hard together to make sure I got through this with them. My first visit with my worker was interesting. She took me out for lunch at a bagel shop, close to Kennedy and 401, to discuss how I was feeling and what was going on in my life. So I told her, Diary, and I told her everything. I really hope you don't judge me, Diary. I know I've said that to you before, but I feel as though I need to say it again, because I am going to tell you more things that I am not proud of, but they've helped me become the woman I am today, so I have no regrets. I am going to lay it all out on the table for you right now. You think my uncle was just my major issue. No, no. There was a lot of shit, man. I don't know why I was so comfortable around her. I didn't know her at all, but she made me feel comfortable. It never felt as if I was talking to a social worker. It felt more like I was talking to a sister, a real sister that really cared about me and wanted to see the best happen for me. Well, you know how I told you my parents separated? I told her that I just wanted to be happy, but I didn't know how to do it. I am so scared, Diary, to tell you everything. I really am. But I need to get everything off my chest and mind in order to grow.

EMERALD

I knew that I didn't want to be in the system or a part of the streets forever. I knew I could be a woman of standards, but how could I do that when I felt so low and hid behind a smile that was fake? Everyone would tell me how beautiful my smile was, so it became my defence mechanism. I was not really happy; I was very sad. I felt alone. Sometimes I even thought about and planned ways to kill myself. Is death easier than life? Life is what I know, Diary. I don't know what death is. I don't even know what it's like. I've only experienced death through the lives I knew that were lost through the streets. That hurt me, and I would cry every time I got sad news. I've heard so many different theories about what happens after you die, and the only way to find out is to actually be dead. I am so scared of myself. Help me!

My life is a hot mess, so I am sorry if this sounds like a rant. I used to be a stripper, and my dance name was Emerald. I did it for almost a year. I would run out of the house late at night with my friends. It got really intense. A man even paid me money so he could perform a sexual act on me. Don't you find that kind of weird? I thought it was supposed to be the other way around, but I didn't really care; I just wanted the money. It was easy for me after the first couple of times. I became numb to it. I didn't feel anything anymore. I looked at it as a business transaction. Honestly, Diary, dancing for money, without having to have sex with these guys, and then when an old man wants to eat your pussy and pay you, how can you really say no? In my opinion, I was winning at that point in my life. Now that I am telling you all of this, I sit here and question myself, "Was I really winning? I was getting money, but was I really winning? What defines winning? What is it, and who measures who wins and who loses?

One night we went out to a strip club to pick up guys. This one guy started talking to my friend, but she didn't want to do anything with him. She sure did want his money, though. So we made him fill up the gas tank. She then asked him for some money upfront as a deposit to book him for the night. Then we just drove off. He chased us on the highway for about forty-five minutes. We drove from Mississauga to Pickering to Scarborough. He even tried to run us off of the highway with his car, to the point where we swerved and almost ran into the guard rail. We then called up some people we knew, and they told us to keep letting him chase us, and to drive to them. I guess the guy must have caught on to what we were trying to do and decided to leave us alone, as he eventually just went the other way.

That's not the only thing I was doing. I used to sell drugs, like real drugs. Crack was selling faster than a Lick's burger on sale, okay. I would sell in the Far East of Ontario. I would stay up there for days at a time. I would stay at what we call a "custies", or crack head's, house and sell crack out of their home, then head back to Toronto to make more before going back. It was business. I had to keep it running. I don't really know why I did all of this. Well, I do, but I didn't realize it back then. I had low self-esteem, but at the same time, I loved doing it, and I thought I was the shit, Diary, and untouchable.

I did this for awhile, until something really fucked-up happened between a friend and me. Something tragic happened, and we fell out and stopped talking. I don't really want to go into detail about it, Diary. Some things are better left unsaid, so I'll just keep it in my mind. Everyone has a dark side and dark secrets that they say they will take to the grave with them. Even though I am writing to you, Diary, I still don't want to say, because I don't know whose hands you could end up in, real talk. Believe it or not, we ended up seeing each other, and

I think we were both prepared for a battle. We ended up reconnecting, but we were hesitant at the same time. We actually ran into each other at Canada's Wonderland one summer, and we reconnected there. As I said, we were both hesitant with each other, but we spoke on and off. I don't remember what exactly happened, but we lost contact again. It wasn't due to anything bad this time.

There is so much more about her, and everything else, that I need to tell you, but there is so much in between that I have to tell you about first, so that you don't get confused. Diary, I hope you can keep up with this. So when my family was threatened, I got a gun and hid it in the house to make sure that if anyone came to harm them or me, I was prepared. I think my mom was catching on to something from time to time, especially when I would just lock myself in my room and not come out. My mom was, and still is, very smart. I swear she knew something was going on with me. She knew something was fucking with me, mentally and emotionally. She and my dad had been on the phone a lot, talking about me. They thought that I didn't know that they were talking about me. They were trying to talk in code. Every time I went into the kitchen, my dad would just look at me and wait for me to leave the kitchen. Diary, if you're going to talk about me, at least try and hide it. My mom started talking to me about going somewhere with her for a period of time, but she wouldn't tell me where exactly. I just listened to her, but I had zero intention of actually following through with her plans. Diary, sometimes you just have to save face and play as if you're listening to your parents.

Diary, I am so pissed right now. Can you believe what my fucking dad did? See, didn't I say my parents thought they were slick? This is going to be a rant, Diary. This man told me that he was leaving me with my aunt for the weekend, but that wasn't the case at all. He never came back. He never fucking came back. He ended up leaving me there and wouldn't answer my motherfucking calls. He would only answer my aunt's calls when she called him from her cell phone. Fuck, man, I had to stay there, and my aunt was extra as fuck sometimes. What the fuck, man? You know what? There was a positive that came out of it, though. I met a guy that lived right by aunt's house. He called my aunt "Mom." We started hanging out, and I would always go over to his house to run away from my aunt and get a break. I swear, she is crazy; I don't give a fuck what anyone says. I felt as if she just had me in her house to talk shit, and then when I did change my life, she played hero and stated that she was the one who saved my life. *Get the fuck out of here with that fake bullshit!*

That guy was so nice to me. We would spend a lot of time together, crack jokes, and have good conversations all day and night. So if I didn't see him for a day, I would automatically know that something was wrong—either the police were on the block or he was laying low. He had family issues, too. We all have family issues, Diary. You're so lucky that the only things you have to share are the other pages and lines in yourself. I didn't see him for several days. I called his phone, and there was no answer. It was off. I was very worried. I thought he had gotten arrested. And just when I said to myself, *"He is probably in jail. I'll just have to wait for him to come out, because I know he will call me,"* this dude showed up at my aunt's house in two casts, a few days later. He told me that he had gotten shot, and I immediately started crying. That's when our relationship started to get deeper, because I realized that I really cared about him, and he cared about me. Well, at least that's what I thought. He got shot in his leg and hand. I had to help feed and bathe him. He was on heavy medication for his pain and swelling. He was taking Percocet and another type of drug to help with the healing process. He wanted to try and see if he could still use both of his legs the same way, so he asked me to go on top of him, and we had sex. It was so funny, but it felt good at the same time. While I was on top of him, I was thinking, *"Yeah, your legs are working just fine."*

LEAVE

☙❧

We continued our relationship. Everything was fine for a little bit, but then we slowly started to drift apart. He wouldn't answer my calls, and took yonder years to call me back. I still went over there to help him. He started giving me excuses, like he was in a lot of pain and was sleeping. I noticed girls going in and out of his mom's house, and every time I showed up there, they would leave right away. I saw that one of the girls changed her name in his phone to "Wifey," with her picture. I questioned him about it, and he denied everything, claiming she was just a friend that liked him, but he had told her that he was in a relationship. Stupid me, I believed him. I then saw another girl starting to come around, but she never stayed very long. I knew in my heart what he was doing, but I just didn't want to listen to my intuition. I wanted to feel wanted still. Diary, every girl's dream is to have a man that wants her and values her, you know. I began distancing myself from him slightly, due to the many females I saw hanging around. He would call me and ask me to come over and bathe him, and I would go over to help him. He was still my man at the end of the day, right? So I had to be there for him, especially considering his situation.

One day while I was bathing him, one of my friends, whom I considered my sister, wanted me to come fight some girls for her at Warden Station. She told me that there were some girls starting problems with her on the train. I was already not in a good mood because of everything that was going on with my boyfriend, so her calling me just got me more amped. I ended up going. When I got there, the girls were gone, but my friend and her friend were in the bathroom getting themselves together. I tried to go looking for those girls, and started to do my research about them. I found out exactly who they were. While I was in the bathroom at the station, I realized my period had come, and I didn't have a pad on me. So I told my friend to come with me to my other friend's house, and then we would deal with the situation from there. Little did I know that my life was about to change forever.

I needed to get a pad that I could change into. When I got to my friend's house, I went to the bathroom right away. When I went to put on the pad, there was no blood there. It was as if my period had done a Harry Houdini trick and disappeared. I thought, *"Oh, fucking shit."* My heart started racing fast. I thought I was going to pass out. So many thoughts were running through my mind. I came out of the bathroom, looked at my friends, and said, "I think I am pregnant." They all looked at me in shock. I took a pregnancy test later on in the week, and it was positive. I immediately went over to my boyfriend's house to tell him the news. I was nervous about telling him, because, as I told you already, we had started getting distant. When I went there, I saw the same girl whom I had seen before. But there were so many females that I'd quarrelled with him about, I couldn't even tell you her name. I told him that I needed to talk to him right away. We went to his grandfather's room, whom I was also close with, and I told him that I was pregnant. I thought his reaction would have been different, but things definitely changed from that point on.

He walked away from me and said that he would talk to me later. That "later" came several days later. I was so irritated with him. When he came over to my aunt's house, he asked how I was doing, and what would happen now. He told me he missed me. He then said that we needed to talk, and that he felt confused, and that there was something that he had to tell me that I was not going to like. When I asked him what it was, he refused to tell me at first. Then he just blurted out to me that we couldn't have this baby, and that he wanted me to have an abortion. I told him that I was scared and didn't want to have one. He understood what I was saying, and he finally decided to come clean about all of his bullshit. His truth finally came out. He told me that he was cheating on me with one of the girls that I kept seeing running out of his mom's house, along with other girls, and that she was pregnant also. I immediately told him to get out of my aunt's house. I was so angry inside. In my head, I thought about all our late-night conversations, all the shit I did to help him after he got shot. I felt betrayed. This motherfucker gave me an ultimatum, and I don't take ultimatums well.

He told me that if he and I work it out, then he would be in our child's life, but if we don't work it out, then he wanted nothing to do with our child. Diary, let me tell you, I may have loved him, but I pressed the exit button really quickly, without looking back. We still spoke, but only to argue about his cheating and getting another woman pregnant. She was three months behind me. Pretty fucked up, yeah, I know. I'm happy that I was smart enough to say goodbye to him. I never saw him or spoke to him after that. I tried to get in contact with him one other time, before I completely stopped talking to him, but he blocked me on Facebook, because all we did was argue on there. Diary, what was I going to do? I was pregnant in my aunt's house, which I thought was crazy. What was I supposed to do now? Was I supposed to have a child with no father? I did not want to be a Black statistic. My family already saw me as the one who was the troublemaker, and now I had to tell them that I was pregnant. I thought to myself, *"Death is much fucking easier than life, but if I kill myself, I won't just be killing me, I would also be killing my unborn child, and that would make me a murderer. Nope, no, thank you."*

BROTHER

I knew I had to move out of her house, because I was pregnant and wasn't in the best environment. I got in touch with the City of Toronto through one of my uncle's ex-wives. She was the one who helped my soon-to-be-child's father get to the hospital, so it still pisses me off that he dissed me the way he did. She introduced me to someone whom I now refer to as my brother, a City of Toronto staff member. He met up with me a few times, and we discussed what was going on as well as the possible next steps that I should take. Diary, a messed-up situation happened, and stuff got really intense in the area. My aunt was also going through some challenges with my uncle, which she usually took out on me and one of my other cousins. One day she was upset at her husband but took it out on me. She picked up the laundry basket that had clothes in it and threw it at me, while I was walking down the stairs. Yes, she knew I was pregnant, but clearly she didn't care. I knew that was my last straw. I called the guy from the City of Toronto, and I showed him what was going on, and that I really needed to get out of there fast. He listened to every word I said and got me out of there in a hurry. He placed me in a residence-shelter for young pregnant moms called Rosalie Hall.

I moved into Rosalie Hall on an emergency basis. He helped me leave my aunt's house. I packed up all of my stuff and left. I was very nervous about moving to a residence, which was just like a shelter to me. Diary, that place changed my life. It really changed my life. Not for the worse, though, but for the better. Remember that everything happens for a reason, and this was for sure a good reason. I met my primary worker. She was so cool, but I was still hesitant and nervous, especially the first couple of weeks. I had to get used to the rules and routines. I lived there for about a year before moving out. It was a life-changing experience for me. I had my probation officer as well as a community service worker who would often come in for meetings to see how I was doing and find out the next steps. They were all supportive of me, and kept it real with me at all times. They told me when I was wrong and when I was right. They helped mould me into not just the woman but also the mother that I was going to become. Don't get me wrong, there were days that I felt guilty for having a baby without the father in my child's life. I felt as though I had failed my child. I would always ask myself at night, *"Why did I choose a man that doesn't want to be a dad?"* I would cry myself to sleep thinking about it. I had the support of the workers, my friends, and some family members. I had to remind myself that God doesn't give us battles we can't handle, and that every child is a blessing.

I didn't speak to my child's father, but he did come there once. He came with one of my cousins. They paged me to the front desk, saying I had visitors. I didn't see him at first, because I just peeped around the corner. I only saw my cousin. I got up and gave my cousin a hug, and that's when I saw him. I was upset, but my cousin encouraged me to listen to him. My cousin told me that they had told him that I was having a boy, and when he found out, he wanted to come see us immediately. He asked me for a hug, and I gave him a very cold hug with no words. He then began telling me and my cousin some bullshit story of how he was so happy that I was having his first boy. However, there was a catch to his foolishness. Diary, he said, "How come I can't have both of you?" Meaning both me and the girl he cheated on me with. I thought to myself, *"Is this guy on some cheap drugs?"* I could clearly tell he hadn't changed one bit. He was still the same old ignorant and selfish son-of-a-bitch individual. I don't even like wasting my time talking about him anymore. Although I was upset with his stupidity, I was happy that he showed up and said what he said. It made me feel good about my decision to leave him. I just figured that he was another woman's problem now, and obviously, he was going to do the same shit to her anyways.

It was funny to me, because shortly after that visit, I found out that not only did he have me and the other girl he cheated on me with pregnant, but he also had two other women pregnant at the time, too. One of them had a miscarriage, and the other one had an abortion. I thanked God that I left that situation alone, and just tried to focus on preparing for my son to enter the world. While I was staying at Rosalie Hall, I began to abuse my body, but in a different way. I just wanted to feel loved and wanted. I wanted a man to appreciate me for who I was and for what I was worth. I was so lonely in there. Diary, did I even know my worth? I know it now, but back then I didn't. A guy started talking to me while I was pregnant. He didn't care that I was pregnant. He always tried to have sex with me, but I refused to. In my head, I was thinking, *"Who in their right mind would want to have sex with a woman that's pregnant for another man? One of those men who would constantly harass my soul."* I ended up in a relationship with him for a little bit. Right before I had the baby, I decided to stop talking to him. He just filled a void for me temporarily.

Diary, I was so depressed. I was emotionally eating. I would eat, eat, and eat some more, and if anybody took my plate away or said I had had enough food, I started bawling right away.

Maybe I was crying too much that day, Diary, because that night I went into labour. I was watching a movie in the living room with a few other girls. I remember feeling really thirsty. The moment I stepped foot into the kitchen, my water broke. I walked into the living room and told the girls, and they looked at me as though I was lying, because I was so calm. My son changed my life so much. He was born on June 13, 2009. Diary, he looked like such an old soul when he was born. His father wasn't there, of course, but I did tell his family friend, who was like a sister to him, that I had the baby. She immediately told me that he looked exactly like his father, which he did. He had the brightest blue eyes, which quickly turned into a green-hazel colour. They looked like cat eyes. He was such a good baby. He would just lay there and coo to himself, and I would thank God for him each day. I would always think to myself, day in and day out, how I was going to make a life for him.

I knew that the first step was leaving Rosalie Hall. They had helped me so much that I became confident in making a plan to move out. I asked my primary worker to help me with the process. I felt like I was outgrowing that place. Diary, other young moms were coming in—not that I am judging them or anything—but each new woman that walked through those doors just seemed ghetto to me. I even got into an argument with two of them and wanted to fight them. The one fight I remember well was when I saw one of the moms cleaning the chicken with dish soap. I was not eating that shit. Luckily, one of the girls that I made a friendship with just reminded me why I was there and my future plans, and I instantly calmed down. I loved being a mom, and I loved being my son's mom even more. I seemed to be adapting just fine to parenthood. The only thing I didn't enjoy was waking up every two hours, but I got used to it. The staff there really helped me cope, and if I was really tired, one of them would stay in my room just to watch him for me. I really appreciated that, Diary. It can be so hard, especially when you're doing it on your own.

BUILDING

I began looking for places, and I remembered that one of my friends that previously lived at Rosalie Hall had moved out to a building that wasn't far from my dad's house. I went to her building and inquired about renting an apartment. Diary, if you think it's easy to just find a place and move out, think the fuck again. There is a process that you have to go through. I had to apply for social assistance, and I applied to housing, which is a program that helps residents with low income, or no income, rent an apartment. Unfortunately, I didn't get the housing before I left, because the waiting list was super long. So I applied for social assistance and moved out. I moved into a building at the corner of Markham and Sheppard, and the funny thing is that I still reside there. I moved into a two-bedroom apartment with a den, just my son and me. He was three months old when I moved in. My friend now became my sugar buddy. That's what they call neighbours, Diary. She and I were very close, and yes, we did some stupid shit together when we were younger, but we were older now and our focus was our children. Everything else came after that. It's interesting how our lives can change so quickly. We went from stealing cars and running dumb girls off the block to becoming responsible mothers for our children. I was happy being a mother, but I still felt lonely at times. I met a guy and, Diary, he was younger than I was, but I thought that I was in love with him. We began our relationship, and both he and his mother accepted my son, and even helped me take care of him. If you're about to get excited for me, Diary, don't. It wasn't what you think. That relationship didn't last long at all. I think the bread in my house survived longer than that.

Diary, it seemed as if I was involved in one problem after another problem after another. I just couldn't catch a fucking break. Here I go again with yet another story of how a past relationship fucked shit up. All I was trying to do was help someone out. I know how it feels to not have any support and to feel beyond alone. One of the young moms that I met at Rosalie Hall needed a place to stay, so I gave her an offer that she could live with me until she got back on her feet. She, her boyfriend, and her child came to live with me. They seemed to get along with my boyfriend, but that didn't last long either. He got into arguments with her boyfriend, and things just went too far. One morning I got up—I was usually the first one to wake up in the house—and I noticed that my front door was left wide opened, and my friend's child was just about to crawl outside into the hallway. I went to grab her and came back inside. That's when I noticed that my boyfriend had stolen my friend's boyfriend's television out of my living room.

I immediately woke them up. I called my boyfriend right away and told him to bring it back, and he denied the entire thing. I didn't know what to do anymore. Obviously, the tension rose between my friend and me, but we were still okay. She then told me that she was going to leave, which I completely understood. Before she left, though, another fucked-up situation happened, and it was because of my boyfriend. Why the fuck did I stay with him? I don't know why I didn't leave him after the first incident. I guess I got used to that lifestyle, and it became the norm for me. I myself wasn't directly involved in it, but I was still attracted to people with negative mentalities. People would always come to my house and stay over. The same friend that I told you lived in my building lent their electronic device to one of my other friends, and my boyfriend took that as well, which caused another problem.

Everyone was trying to warn me that eventually he would do the same to me, but I didn't listen to them, and I continued being with him. We got into a really big fight, and I got a knife, but I didn't do anything to him. He grabbed the knife from me while I was cornered in the kitchen, and in the process of taking the knife from me, he cut himself. He was already mad, but his anger skyrocketed after that. He and I got into a physical fight. I backed down immediately, because I didn't want to fight with my son there. I had grabbed the knife because I was scared. We ended up fighting anyways. He punched me in my temple, and I remember feeling really dizzy, and that brought me down to the floor slowly. I felt dizzy after that. I banged my head on my son's highchair, causing my head to split open and bleed right above my right eye. My entire face was covered in blood. Diary, have you ever been licked on the face by a dog, then all the saliva hardens on your face? Well, that's how it felt. There was so much blood. I called my friend, and she came over right away. She helped clean up the blood on the floor, and helped me clean off my face. I felt light-headed. My mother had bought me a laptop, and before he left, he took that, too. I kept calling him, and he said that he was going to return it, but he never did. I already had the Children's Aid Society in my life, because I had lived in a young women's residence while having a baby, and they were just an added support. To be honest,

Diary, a lot of people think negatively about the society, and I do as well. Not because I was involved with them; they were never worried about me. It was more because I had charges and shit. My worker and I built a good relationship.

It's now that I feel that the society is failing these youths, especially the vulnerable ones. They found out what happened, and they ordered that I was not to be around him, and he could not be anywhere near my son. I was fine with that. The police had to get involved because of that incident as well. I went to court, and all that happened was that he gave me the money for the laptop. That was the last time I spoke to him. I saw him after that, about a year or two later. It was awkward at first, but there was no bad blood between us, which was good. I tried to move on with my life, which I did.

Diary, sometimes it is good to just take a step back and re-evaluate your life, your goals, your wants, and your needs. You also have to ask yourself if you've even been trying to work towards your goals. Diary, I can tell you straight up that I wasn't. I was so focused on other people that I didn't even think of investing in myself. I just wanted someone to love me and give me attention. I wanted a companion, someone to share my life with, but I didn't seem to have any luck in that department. I was lonely, and I began to feel sad all the time. The only time I would smile was when I would see my son smile. He was honestly such a good baby. He barely cried. He loved just chilling on my lap and watching TV. And he loved food. I love food, too, so I knew he was my child.

TIMING

The good thing is that when you get used to being alone, which I did, it becomes normal, and you realize that the person you left, or who left you, was just a phase in your life and a lesson learned. I came to understand that my time would come to give and receive true love, so not to push anything, just to let it happen, let it flow. That's exactly what I did, and I think I found, well I should say reconnected with, my soul mate one January afternoon. My friend invited me to her son's first birthday party in the west end of Toronto. Diary, I had no intention of going, because I wasn't feeling like myself, and I still had my down days. I am only human. I had to go, though. She was like my little sister. Diary, Rosalie Hall connected me to a couple of lifelong friends. I still talk to her to this day. I will always talk to her. She is a really good mom, and she is still finding herself as well. It makes me feel good that she looks up to me. That must mean I do have good things about me. I do have strong qualities that I hold in high esteem. I just misplaced them on the wrong people.

There is saying, "You don't know unless you try." So I left to go have fun with the kids and my friends. When I got on the bus, I got reconnected with the person I think is my soul mate. I met him in 2006, by Midland and Lawrence, at a gas station. Little did I know that he was about to become the love of my life. We began hanging out almost every day. He then got his car and began dropping off my son to daycare with me and then driving me to work. I introduced him to my friends and the friends I call family, two of whom were my son's godmothers. I'll get to "were" later. I called them my cousins; well, one of them was an issue. They got along well with him, and he hung out with us all the time. I was suspicious of one of them, because she would always say he reminded her of an ex-boyfriend that she was still in love with from the States. Anyways, I didn't really let that get to me too much, because I started to trust him.

Diary, I swear I just wrote this to you. I couldn't catch a fucking break. I was exhausted. I just wanted to cry. I was done. I understood why people killed themselves, I really did. Over the next little while, I started to experience back pain, intense pelvic pain, and I felt very sick. I would take Advil, and I smoked weed for the most part, to ease the pain. One afternoon, I was walking inside Scarborough Town Centre with one of my son's godmothers, when all of a sudden I felt a sharp pain run down my right leg. It started from around my hip. I started struggling to walk. I felt as if she and I were fake friends, but at least I wasn't alone in that situation. She took me to the clinic right outside the mall, and they brought me in immediately. They told me that I needed to go to the hospital and be admitted. I was admitted to Scarborough General Hospital.

Diary, that's when I found out I had cervical cancer. If things weren't already bad, they only got worse as that day went by. The same girl I told you I felt was only my fake friend went to my boyfriend's workplace and told him not to come to the hospital to see me, that I was cheating on him with my ex, and that I had a sexually transmitted disease. I am happy that he never listened to her and came regardless. When he got to the hospital, I could tell he was upset, and I asked what was wrong with him. He said to me, "Just because you don't see me crying now doesn't mean that I wasn't." Remember, Diary, I didn't know that she had gone to tell him all the bullshit yet. He was the reason I found out everything. I asked him what he was talking about, and I encouraged him to talk to me about whatever was on his mind. He then told me what she had said. It's a good thing I was on the floor where cancer patients were, so he knew I wasn't lying about that. However, I did do something wrong. I had lied to him about my age, because I didn't want him to take advantage of me. I told him I was twenty, when I was really nineteen. He was mad about that, but he did stay by my side the entire night.

I stayed in the hospital for about five days, and he was the one that picked me up and brought me home. He even took me to go pick up the medication that my doctor prescribed for me. Before I get to what happened with her afterwards, I will say this, Diary: If you were real and you were a woman that had a child, it is very important to go do your check-up after six weeks of having a baby. I didn't go, or I would have found out way sooner than I did. According to the doctors, it is very common for women to find out that they have cervical cancer, and there is a procedure that they do that burns the cells around the cervix. It was important to the nurses and doctor at the time to just get my pain under control as fast as they could. I swear, one side of my body felt as though it were on fire. Now that I have told you about the procedure and what had to be done, I can get to the "as for her" part. She and I stopped talking immediately, and I began to believe that she was the reason something happened to me on one of my birthdays. Diary, I hate talking about it. It still fucks with my mind and my emotions, till this very day as I write to you.

The only reason why I am going to write about it now is because I am trying to rise behind my blinded eyes. I regret not listening to my parents and my brother. I hope you can handle what I am saying, and, Diary, I pray that nobody else finds you and reads this. If they do, you better do some kind of magic trick and change each page as they read it. For one of my birthdays, I was talking to a guy that I had met in the west end. I met his friends, and they seemed cool. The bitch that I stopped talking to also said that she used to talk to one of his friends, but didn't want me to say anything, which I found weird, but whatever. Moving on from that thought, one of his friends messaged me on Facebook and made it seem as if they were throwing a party for me, so I obviously invited my friend, and she came with me. I thought that the guy that I was talking to was going to be there. When I got there, he was nowhere to be found, but I wasn't bothered yet, because it came off to me as a surprise party.

I asked all of them where he was immediately, and they said to me that he was on the way. They all seemed very relaxed and fun. I didn't think anything was wrong. I hate calling her my friend, but since I am telling you the story, I have to refer to her as my friend. I started drinking and enjoying myself, when randomly she said she was going to the store to get a cake for me. Up until this day, I haven't seen a cake. While she was gone, things took a turn for the worse, and fast. I remember some pieces, but the majority of it is a blur to me. I remember stairs and stumbling, but I couldn't tell you if I was walking up or down the stairs. My body felt very limp and weak. I could barely even talk. I remember hearing one of the guys laughing and saying, "She doesn't even know what is about to happen," and he continued laughing. I was now in the bathroom. One guy at a time took off my clothes. One began fucking me, one tried putting his dick in my mouth, and I remember crying and screaming, but it was very faint. I was so weak. I said to one of them, "How could you do this to me? Get off of me!" I said that to the guy that my boyfriend considered to be his best friend.

EXPLOITED

I remember seeing more than one person, but I could not make out their faces, and then after that I don't remember anything at all. I couldn't fight any of them off, because I was so weak. I just remember crying. I could hear them walking me to the balcony. They were holding me up, because I couldn't walk. Diary, for a second, I thought they were going to throw me over the balcony. I heard one of the guys say, "You better tell her my name is Bob, because I am not involved in this." Diary, I still get flashbacks about that day, and when I get them, they're very vivid, as if I am reliving it all over again. She finally came back to the house, and I remember her yelling at them and screaming, "What did you do to her? Why is there sperm all over my cousin?" None of them answered her. All they told her was that they didn't know what she was talking about. She found me lying on the bathroom floor, passed out. She woke me up with water, cleaned me off, and walked me to the car. She didn't even find all of my clothes.

In the car, I kept dozing in and out. She was panicking and calling people. She called her mom, yelling for her to come outside when we got to her house. Apparently,

I had a seizure, and the next time I woke up, I was in the hospital with two police officers, one detective, and my family members surrounding me. I started crying immediately. I just wanted to go home. The doctor came in and told me that I could have died. He told me that I was hypoglycemic, had been raped, drugged with ecstasy, and that my eyes were six times dilated in size. The doctor also told me that according to my toxicology report there was also something in my system that has the same ingredient found in Drano. Diary, Drano is a drain cleaning product that unclogs pipes.

I just cried. I thought I felt my brother and dad hugging me, but I don't even remember if that actually happened. I do remember my brother encouraging me to talk to the female police officer. The guy that I was talking to at the time had no idea there was even a party. He didn't know anything. The police told me that they had police cruisers outside the house where I was, and were just waiting for me to say that I wanted to press charges. I didn't press charges, though. I was in denial, and I didn't want any problems with anybody in the streets. You can get killed for shit like that. With that being said, the police didn't believe that the girl went to Dairy Queen either. They believed that she set me up, but my dumb ass defended her, because I couldn't believe that she would ever do something like that to me.

Now, after the entire situation with my boyfriend, I look back and realize that she wasn't a real friend at all, and something just doesn't sit well with me about her involvement in my entire birthday event. Yes, in case you're wondering, the answer is yes, I did tell my boyfriend everything that I had gone through. My cervical cancer wasn't a big issue. Yes, cancer is a huge issue; however, they just had to do a procedure where they burn the cells. I was sent home. I had to go back for routine check-ups further along. I was okay, just really worried whenever I would feel pain. Whenever you experience something like that, you always worry, even if it's the slightest pain. I was thankful for my boyfriend. I never felt as though he judged me. Have you ever looked at someone and know that they've gone through shit, too, and they're just waiting to warm up to you to tell you? Well, that's the feeling I got with him.

Our official date for the beginning of our relationship was March 5, 2010. By this time, when everything happened, it was June. Our relationship was still going well. We had sex several times. The first couple of times, we obviously used protection. It's always weird the first couple of times you have sex with someone new, but as you two grow together, you become more comfortable, and it becomes easier as time goes by. Once we felt more comfortable with each other, and established that we were in a committed relationship, we stopped using protection. Diary, I know you might be thinking, "Oh, boy. No, no, no, no, no, no." Don't worry, Diary. But, Diary, your worry was fucking correct, man. I found out I was pregnant about three months into our relationship. I thought he would be happy, but he wasn't. He told me that I should have an abortion, because he wanted me to finish school. I knew that there was something more to it, but because of the situation at hand, I couldn't bother to investigate.

DECISION

He had driven one of my friends somewhere, and I asked her, with him in the car, "What would you do if you were in a relationship with a guy, and you both knowingly never used protection, and then he got you pregnant and told you to have an abortion?" Her response was something along the lines of "He doesn't care about you." I just looked over at him, then looked straight, while he continued driving. I didn't let her know that I was talking about him. I was in my first year of college, completing the Child and Youth Worker program. I was very upset. We spoke about it several times. I even spoke to his sister about it. She told me to keep the baby. In the meantime, while contemplating what to do, he and I got into several arguments.

I would go through his phone all the time, and I kept finding females that he was texting. He was still entertaining one of his children's mother, and was talking to girls about having sex. I saw pictures of him with girls. I was just pissed off by this point. Diary, you already know I didn't leave him, so don't wait for me to say that. We spoke about the baby, and one day, when

I got really upset, I finally agreed with him and called my doctor. I was sixteen weeks pregnant. My doctor referred me to an abortion clinic downtown. I was scheduled to have my abortion on September 24, 2010. Diary, I was so far along that they had to insert two tents inside of me. Tents open up your cervix and make it start dilating. By the time I had the abortion, I was nineteen weeks pregnant, which is approximately five months pregnant. He didn't come with me on that day, because one of his close family friends had passed away due to gun violence. I understood the situation. I told him to go be with them, and he could be with me on the day of the actual abortion. It was a two-day procedure. On the first day, I had to get the tents, and then the second day was the actual abortion.

On my way downtown, I had to stop before I got on the train, to throw up. I kept calling him and calling him and calling him. He never fucking answered his phone. When I got to the abortion clinic, it was as if one of the nurses knew I didn't want to go through with it. The nurse brought me downstairs and asked me several times, "Are you sure that you want to do this?" She was making sure I wasn't being forced to do it. It was as if she could read what I was feeling. I really didn't want to do it. I wanted to run away, but I knew it was too late, especially after the tents were put in. The clinic tried to get in contact with him, and he still wasn't answering. It was time to get the abortion done. I went upstairs into a room. I had to go on IV. They put a drug through it that made me feel drunk. The doctor told me not to cry, because it just makes the situation harder. There were at least five people in the room to assist with the abortion. There was a nurse that stood by my head while I was lying there on the table, to ensure that I was okay. They spoke about celebrities and some other random shit while the procedure was taking place.

They were laughing with each other. I found it weird, and not normal. Diary, why were people laughing around me while I was going through an abortion? Please answer that for me. The procedure took about forty-five minutes. I wanted to cry so badly while lying on that table and hearing the machine and seeing the blood. It was disgusting. I wanted to throw up. Then I went into the waiting room, where they gave me a heating pad, pain medication, and cookies. They kept trying to get a hold of my partner, which they finally did after many tries. He told them that he was sleeping. I wasn't allowed to leave the clinic, unless someone was there to pick me up. He got there about two hours after they spoke to him. He seemed hesitant to talk to me, and seemed unsure of what I was going to say. We were told that since the baby was so far along, we could have a burial for him. Diary, it was a baby boy. So that's what we did. We planned for one, and it was hard for me. I didn't think it would be, especially after it was done, but it was hard.

I spoke to his sister shortly after I had the abortion. I told her that I had one and, Diary, that's when our relationship took a dramatic turn for the worse. She told me all kinds of foolishness, like "God is watching you," while defending her brother's other baby mothers, stating that they kept all his kids. Little did she know the full truth, but it wasn't my place to tell her. She just kept it coming. She even had her child call me and explain to me why she was upset and didn't want to talk to me anymore, as if I gave a fuck at this point. I began to develop a real hate for her, because she didn't know shit about what she was speaking on. That's usually how it goes—people speak on other people's situations, without knowing the full story. I was crying a lot. I hated him and blamed him for all the drama. Our son was buried on October 5, 2010. He and I got into an argument, and guess what, he never came at all. I had to do it and go through it all on my own. So now my hatred for him started turning into resentment. I felt as if he was taking advantage of my love and was just using me. The same shit kept happening, over and over. He entertained woman after woman.

Everyone started asking me why I stayed with him, and the only reason I could really come up with was that I loved him and that I saw something in him, which I truly did. I know it sounds like I am defending him, Diary, but he is not a bad person. He is a very funny person. I just figured he needed to grow up and handle his shit like a man. I went into depression after that, and had a seizure at school due to all the stress. All he did was call. He was never there for me. I was beginning to think he was either messing around with other women or he was still fooling around with a woman from his past. The same shit, Diary, the same fucking women shit. We stayed together, though, and I know you're getting mad at me now. I started getting mad at the fact that he would never defend me to anybody, and that he was entertaining one of his exes' bullshit. Well, that's at least what it seemed like. One of his children eventually started living with him.

He introduced me to the child, and we went downtown together for some fun. Since his child was now living with him, he needed help with getting the child situated in school, among other things. He enrolled the child in the same daycare as my son, so that it would be easier, not only for him, but for me also. When school came around, it was as if I wasn't even living at my house. From Sunday to Friday, I was at his house. It was okay. I got to see him every day. I thought that everything was okay with our relationship. However, Diary, I was wrong. He continued entertaining women, and now it was getting to me. One of his exes actually called and told me she was pregnant with his child, and that they were still sleeping together. As soon as she told me that, I went outside to him, where he was talking to one of his friends, and I started yelling at him. His friend left, and then I chased him down the street, screaming. We ended up in the house again, and eventually calmed down and talked to each other. He denied everything. The hardest part was I knew was still in love with him, but then again, he seemed to love the attention that he was getting. That night went by, and I began to think to myself that I was just breaking my own heart by staying with him, but I never left. He changed for a week, maybe two.

He became a loving man. I remembered why I fell in love with him. He was everything that I ever wanted in a man, and I was happy that I never decided to give up on him. It seemed that every argument we got into, he would go right back to being an asshole, Diary. It was as if he looked forward to us having rough times so that he could go out there and entertain women. I still managed to keep on top of my school work, no matter what was going on between us. I was practically living with him at this point. I was stupid, like dumbass stupid, Diary, for his love. I allowed him to take advantage of my love for him, time after time. The smallest gestures of kindness would satisfy me immensely. Remember, Diary, I am not trying to make an excuse for myself, but I never knew what love was. I couldn't tell you how it felt.

UNIFICATION

☙❧

Diary, you won't believe this. On January 1, 2012, he asked me to marry him. I was beyond happy. I could have gone outside and screamed "I loved him!" to the world. Diary, you just don't understand. I know you're confused as fuck right now, with all the ups and downs. The connection that he and I shared was absolutely incredible. I fell as if the world was revolving around us each time. I fell in love with him all over again. Before he asked me to marry him, I remember him talking to me about our relationship and what I meant to him. I was literally lost in his words and in his eyes. The love we shared was so strong that a stranger could walk in and feel it at that very moment. Everything was great for a bit, and you already know what I am going to write, Diary. I swear, you're going to throw yourself away if I write this one more time to you. The same shit happened, but this time it wasn't just entertaining. He actually cheated. Well, this was the first time it had been confirmed that he actually slept with someone.

He cheated with someone from his past on August 3, 2012. Yes, Diary, I remember that date. Anyone would remember a date that they were really hurt on, or that is really important to them. Let me tell you how it went down. I woke up that morning and saw the change in his status very early in the morning, which was very unusual. I called the girl and spoke to her. She said he was probably with some other woman, because he wasn't there at that moment. So I called the other ex, and she told me that he had just left from her house and that they had had sex. I then called him, and he admitted it, but not right away. I was so upset. I called my friend crying, and she picked me up in the middle of the road, because I was busy screaming at him on the phone, to the point where she got out of the car, grabbed my phone, and directed me straight to her car.

Diary, this fucking man had the nerve to say some dumb shit. This man told me, "Don't cry over spilt milk," and brushed it off as if it wasn't a big deal. I was so flipping mad. He even had the nerve to entertain the bitch the next day when she was calling him and messaging him, saying that was the best sex she had had in a long time. He was laughing about it right in front of me. As I am writing this to you, I realize how ridiculous I sound for even thinking of staying with him after all of that. That still didn't make me leave him, and up until now, I have no idea why I stayed. Diary, if he was any of my other exes, I would have left his ass a very long time ago. Was it still love? Was it just plain stupidity? Or had I fallen so hard for him that I had lost myself? I personally think it was all three of the above. We made up the next night. He didn't want to have sex with me, because he said it didn't feel right. He didn't want me to feel as though he was using me. I swear, he knew exactly what to say and when to say it. His apology, Diary, felt so sincere.

While we were having sex, the feeling I told you about when he asked me to marry him consumed both of us so strongly that we had to stop and just look at each other and embrace. He even said, "Christene, I never gave her this. I never gave her what we share." That night was so passionate, and it continued even into the next morning. We became inseparable for awhile, and our communication improved. However, Diary, I found out something about myself when it came to him. I had to keep lying to him for him to show me love and attention. I would tell him I was not feeling well, when I was actually feeling fine, just because I wanted him around. He was never there. Phone calls and texts were just not enough, especially when I wanted something real. I actually wanted to build with someone. I wanted to build with him. He was so inconsistent with his love for me. It's not to say I wanted revenge, but I was just tired of giving somebody my all and doing everything for them, just to get nothing in return. When I say that, I don't mean money, Diary. I mean loyalty, love, and commitment. For fuck's sake, the man asked me to marry him. You would think he would've straightened up by now, but no. Let me make this very clear to you, Diary.

I know that this is hard to believe right now, but he is a good person. That's why I refused to give up on him. He is amazing, and I loved him through it all. Regardless of how stupid of a girl I sound, Diary, I told you earlier that I started to think about revenge. I wanted to play his game. I wanted him to feel how I felt. Diary, there is a saying that men can't handle the pain they put us through, eh. I began flirting with guys. Hey, at the end of the day, they were making me smile, and he wasn't. I was tired of crying. Around November of 2012, we found out that he was going to jail, only on weekends though, for some old shit. It was sad that I didn't have him for the weekends, but I had him during the week. It was bad, but it wasn't the worst. I would usually stay around his friends on the weekend, or by his mother's, just to give him some peace of mind, because boy, he was quick to accuse me of cheating on him. I was so excited to see him each Monday morning that he came out. On the last weekend that he had to serve, I was so happy. I remember him sitting on his bed, playing video games, and I just laid there watching him. But his attitude began to change. He began making me feel as if I was a bitch to him. I was loving towards him, but he dealt with me like a real thug, as if I was just another notch on his belt.

Shortly after he finished his last weekend in jail, I got into a car accident with a friend, on our way to placement. Placement is something that you have to do while you're in college. It helps you gain experience in the career field that you want to pursue. He definitely showed his concern with his words, but not with his actions. I was walking with a cane, and I had a brace on my arm. I struggled to do my hair, buy groceries, and do certain things for my son. Diary, you never know how strong you are until you have to do things completely on your own, no matter the situation and no matter who you think is in your corner, or is supposed to be there. He wasn't there to help me with anything. Our relationship began to slide, again. I would call him every day while he was on his way to work, and I would tell him that I loved him and that I didn't want to give up on us. I was scared that I was losing him. He continued to brush me off as though I didn't mean anything to him. I began to talk to another man. He made me feel special, liked, and important. We began talking every morning at work; he always had time for me.

Yes, I know what I was doing was wrong, and I have no excuse for it. But, Diary, that's not all that happened. I was so tired of his shit. Just hold tight, let me finish. Diary, keep up. One night he planned to come over. He probably thought he was coming to have sex, but I had zero intention of doing so. He came really late, like around two in the morning or so. When he came to my door, he seemed apprehensive and kept looking behind him. I asked him if everything was okay. He said "yes" and continued inside. We sat on the couch and watched TV, and he laid down on my lap. I started getting phone calls from my man, or whatever you want to call him at this point. I felt as if we weren't together, to be honest. Text messages and calls kept coming in. I didn't answer him at first, but something just seemed very odd, especially the fact that when I opened my door to this guy, he seemed concerned. I finally read the text messages. He and the guy had taken the elevator together, and he saw him come to my door. He said that he couldn't even blame me, because it was his fault, but he kept saying a whole bunch of shit. I lied to him and told him he was my cousin. That was the quickest lie I could come up with, and I thought it would work, because the guy and I had the same last name. I was scared, Diary. I didn't want him coming to my house to start any shit. I eventually told the guy to leave, and I even walked him downstairs to his car, just to make sure he got there safely.

I really can't remember if my man came up to my house after that, to be honest. I do know that he saw me downstairs, though, because he sent a sarcastic text, letting me know that he saw me walk this guy downstairs. I thought to myself, "If I was unsure if we were together before, then we definitely weren't together now." Diary, we stayed up all night on the phone, arguing about our relationship and where it had gone wrong. It seemed we knew how to communicate really well when shit hit the fan with us. We talked all day and all night. We told each other we still loved each other, and everything.

Diary, do you know that the guy told people how he and I had sex? We didn't. We had kissed and made out, but we never had sex. I can put that on anything. I had to prove it. I had a friend on a three-way call with him when I confronted him about saying we had sex. I had to make her hear that I didn't sleep with this guy. Till this day, I don't know if she truly believes me that I never had sex with him, but I did try and prove myself.

BLURRY

On Christmas day, my man came over a little late with one of his children to spend time with me and talk about the situation between us and what happened that night when he caught the guy at my house. Shit turned really bad, really quickly. I felt as if I were in a movie because of how fast the events unfolded. He took my phone and went through it. He saw my text to one of my friends, saying, "I think it's too late for me and him." He immediately got upset and told me to go to my room. We went aggressively and left the kids in the living room. I was scared as fuck, because I didn't know what was about to happen. As soon as I went into my room, he grabbed me and pushed me towards the bed. I caught myself, so I didn't fall right away. He then swung with his fist towards me, and he hit me directly in my eye. I fell onto my bed and started covering my face, crying and rolling back and forth, screaming repeatedly, "I can't believe you hit me! You said you'd never do that to me." He was still very angry, and he said he was going to light me on fire. At this point, he still didn't realize what he had done to me. He then realized that something was wrong with me, because I wouldn't get up. I just kept rolling back and forth, covering my face, and crying.

Diary, the man that I loved put his hands on me. I forget what the movie is called, but I felt as if I were in the movie where a guy and his girlfriend were arguing, and it got physical, and the guy didn't know that he had hit his girlfriend. *Baby Boy*, Diary, the movie is *Baby Boy*. I felt so sad. I wasn't even angry with him; I was more hurt and sad than anything. He turned from angry to concerned, in a blink of an eye. He tried to pull my hand away from my face to get my attention and to see what was wrong. I told him to leave my house and not to touch me, and I continued crying and rocking on my bed. He didn't leave, though. He stayed right there. He realized what he had done to my eye. My eye was black and blue and really swollen. I couldn't see through it at all. I looked like Quasimodo. He said "sorry" to me quickly, and gave me a hug, and began crying. I forgave him, Diary, and I tried to console him. At that point, I just wanted him to stop crying. I had never seen him cry before then. It reminded me that he was still human, and we make mistakes. I let him know that I wouldn't leave him and that I'd be there through it all. He wanted to run himself into the police station right after. I begged him not to. He said he even wanted to jump off the balcony. He couldn't believe what he had done to me.

So many emotions and questions were running through my mind. One thing I knew for sure was that I couldn't let the kids see me like this, especially my child. He got ice for my eye, and I wore glasses. I wore sunglasses for about a week. It was really bad. I would walk into the wall when turning the corner, because I couldn't see. Once, I was holding the door open for my son to go through the door, and I accidentally released the door on him. He wasn't hurt, though. That just let me realize how swollen my eye really was, because I couldn't see properly. Diary, I said to myself, "If he hit me once, he can do it again. That means he has gotten over the fear of hitting me. That means he will do it again, especially if I stay." Diary, I convinced myself that my gut was wrong and that I was just thinking crazy. I am going to sound crazy when I say this: I was kind of happy that that day happened, because everything I ever saw in him came out. I saw the love he had for me. I saw the unselfish person in him. I saw everything in him. He didn't want me to go outside at all, until my face was healed. He brought me to his mother's house that night. I came up with a lie to cover for him. He was shocked that I even did that for him. He wanted to go tell his mother what he had done.

He took care of me, brought my son to daycare, and picked him up before he went to work. He took time off work just to spend with me. We went everywhere together. We went downtown together, went out to eat, talked and enjoyed each other. It was really nice. I felt the love between us, again. People wanted our relationship, without knowing the details of our package. I was proud to say that he was my man. I never had a feeling or thought that he was talking to anybody else. I felt like a queen, and that was because of him. We stayed up throughout a lot of nights, talking. I remember one night he came home late from work, and as soon as the bedroom door opened, I jumped into his arms and hugged him. As I write that to you, Diary, I can still feel the feeling of love run throughout my body. It was as if we were enjoying marital bliss. The first words out of his mouth were, "Now this is love. I love you, too." And he hugged me back. It was all good, until we got into an argument. It seemed that everything we had talked about went right out the window. He was that asshole, again. I never gave up on him, though, because I knew who he could really be. I knew the man that he could become. I knew the man I saw in him before he hit me. I knew it all. I knew my love for him could change him. I was not going to give up on him that easily. I had to keep going. And I still had to focus on school and my son.

I was in my second year of school, and it was the hardest. I didn't even get to see my son much, because of my placement. I saw him on Saturdays and Sundays, and then he was gone for the rest of the week. My man was my strength. Well, my love for him was my strength, and the love I have for my son was my strength and motivation to keep going. He would stay up late with me at night when I had to get my assignments done. He would lie between my legs while I was reading my books and studying. Everything wasn't always bad, but I'll admit that the bad did outweigh the good. I knew that things needed to change, especially if we were going to get married and raise a family together, a blended family at that. We had to be the foundation for our children and show them what love really looked like. If we didn't, then the cycle of broken homes would just continue. I wanted to raise our sons to become kings, and our daughters to become queens.

School was good. I was always doing well in my placement and in my academics. I needed to stay focused and on top of my game. I wasn't going to let anyone think that I was a failure. I especially wanted to prove my uncle wrong, and no, I am not talking about the one that molested me. I'm talking about the uncle who said to me that the only thing that I would be smart enough to do was lay on my back. I hated him for that, and I still do. He was fucked-up in my eyes. He became less than the dirt under my shoe after a rainy day. I never told my dad what he said to me, Diary, until I was much older, but I did make it obvious that I did not like him at all. I wanted that money, but better yet, I wanted to look in his face and ask him, "What was the smartest thing you said I was capable of doing?" Diary, I know you can't answer me, but have you ever felt as if someone's negativity towards you drives you harder to reach your goals faster than someone's positivity? Why is that? One thing I do know is that I am proud of myself for finally getting my story out. I was talking about this for years. I was supposed to be finished telling this story years ago. I fell off. I got lazy. I let life discourage me. I was really depressed and at my lowest in life for years.

To be honest, I still think I am a bit depressed, but now I am doing something about it, so I don't feel the effects that I used to. You would be very proud of me. I graduated from Centennial College in 2013. It was amazing. My mom and stepdad came as well as my fiancé. My dad couldn't come, because he was in the hospital. I went directly there after my ceremony. When I walked into his room, I cried while I gave him a hug. He was so proud of me. I could see the glow in his eyes, but at the same time, I could see the sadness because he wasn't able to attend. I know he would have been there screaming my name. He would've probably yelled out my old nickname, which was Snypz. That name was given to me in high school, because I was always on the defence, and very quick to fight and do other shit. I was a fight-first-talk-later kind of person. My mom and stepdad took us all out to Mandarin after my graduation to celebrate. My fiancé, mom, stepdad, brother, sister-in-law, and basically all of my immediately family was there. It was so good, and everyone was very proud of me.

NEW

☙❧

I know some of my family members thought that I was never going to turn my life around, and I do understand why they thought that. I was just happy to prove them wrong, but in a good way, and to thank them, because even if they had doubts, they still never gave up on me. Oh my, I didn't even tell you the best part of my graduation, Diary. I am so sorry. LET ME TELL YOU. LET ME TELL YOU. I AM SO FRIGGING EXCITED. I had applied for a job as a Child and Youth Worker for the Toronto District School Board, and got called for an interview. Guess what? I got the job, and I got it before I even graduated. All I had to do was get my transcripts to show that I would be graduating, my CPR card, and a few other documents. I felt as if I had accomplished my dream. I was nervous. The interview was intense, but easy at the same time. Intense, because it was me and two principals sitting across from me, check-marking and writing down everything I said. They barely made eye contact with me. The questions were scenarios and problem-solving strategies that we would use throughout the field. I got hired and was able to work before that school year was finished in 2013. It was a good experience. I got to work at a school that had a behavioural program, and another school that had an autism program.

A lot of people don't understand the difference. Some people think that people with autism are just behavioural. I guess that's why they have child and youth workers, like me, who can see life through their lens and help them. We all learn differently, depending on the subject at hand; for instance, English. This may sound weird, but in order to grasp and understand what the teacher was trying to teach me, I would have to do it myself. I would have to hear exactly what the teacher was saying, and if it didn't add up or if they missed a step, I would become very confused, and I would often call them out on it. In a polite way, of course. As a student, it always feels nice when you correct your teacher, and you are actually right. I was what you'd call a hands-on learner. When it came to math, I understood it much better when it was repeated several times, over and over. For math, I can say I was an auditory learner. While I was in school, my teachers never understood me at all. My mom always thought I wasn't being challenged enough, and that's why I gave up so easily and caused so much trouble, both in elementary school and high school.

I couldn't stand my teacher. It seemed half of them just taught from a book and not from their hearts. You have to have a passion for what you want to do, if you're serious about actually doing it and doing it right.

Finally, as a Child and Youth Worker, I was happy. I felt as if my life was actually starting to make sense. I felt important, I felt valued, and I felt heard. I felt heard by others who never saw me. For once, I felt as if they could see me, beyond my colour, my struggles, and, more importantly, my mistakes. Things were starting to fall into place. Diary, we were also planning our wedding, which I was very excited about. We had our wedding date set for November 27, 2014, back home in Jamaica. We were both excited and nervous at the same time. Marriage is a big step. Let me take that back. I know I was looking forward to it. I just also got the vibe that he was pretending. I know I had my doubts in my head due to past shit, but I was ready to move forward, and I honestly thought he was ready, too.

I got our wedding invitations created in Markham. They were beautiful. The design on them was a passport design, with the colours purple and gold. It said "International Love Affair" on them. We agreed on a price and agreed to go half and half on them. He told me that he didn't get paid that week, which was a damn lie, because I knew when he got paid. Come on, we'd been together for four years already; I obviously knew a lot about him. I confronted him about it, and he told me that he had lied to me because he wanted to do some stuff for his car. I was so upset and hurt, Diary. This was our fucking wedding. He couldn't even drive at that time anyways. I felt betrayed. He didn't seem interested in the wedding whenever he and I spoke about it, but I continued telling everybody about the wedding.

I just didn't get, but I do know that I was really hurt, and I cried, but not to him. He just laughed it off and never mentioned it again. We stopped planning the wedding after that, and a lot of people lost respect for him because of it. But who cares about the other people. The most important part was that I started to lose respect for him, and respect for us as a couple. I felt as if I had been hung out to dry, with no explanation. I felt stuck in a situation, with no answers or sightlines indicating what our next move was. I started to feel as if he was becoming my enemy. A lot of the past started to come back into my mind. There was a time when we got into an argument, and he was trying to explain himself. In doing that, he said to me, "I am a selfish person, and maybe the only reason why I asked you to marry me was because it was something that I wanted to do before I died." I kept replaying that in my head, over and over and over again. I wondered if this man really loved me.

I couldn't dwell on it forever. I had to move on from it, but trust and believe me, it was hard. I wanted to hurt him and make him feel the hurt that I felt. Diary, I still loved him, but I just didn't know what to do anymore. We continued our relationship; it never ended. It was back to the usual—good one week, fight the next week, make up for about another week, maybe two. It was a cycle, and I was getting tired of it. He had his shit to handle in his personal life, but he never had to do it alone. I never made him go through it alone, but he made me feel as if I was going through a lot of battles, challenges, and struggles on my own. He never had my back the way I had his, Diary. I still cry about this shit. He wasn't even there to give me emotional support. I was just fucking exhausted, Diary.

May came around, and I wasn't feeling myself. I was always tired. I didn't have an appetite, though usually I loved to eat my food. It was odd to me. Then I realized, Diary, that I hadn't gotten my period. So I got a pregnancy test. That bad boy turned positive within seconds. I told him right away. He gave me a reaction that I wasn't expecting at all. I called him, and he was in the car with one of his friends. I said, "Guess what, Daddy?" And he said, "What?" I repeated myself. He had no idea what I was talking about, because there were times when I called him Daddy. I had to switch up my tone. When he finally realized what I was trying to tell him, he was so happy. I was happy, too. From the moment I found out I was pregnant, I felt that it was another boy, because I had the same symptoms as I was having with the first one. I told him that if it was a boy, then we could name him after him, because that was something that I knew he had always wanted. Diary, I looked at it like if I was going to be his wife, then I should be the one to give him his dream. I was right, by the way. It was a boy. I was due January 9, 2015. My pregnancy, for the most part, was okay. However, I did end up in the hospital for about a week due to bleeding when I was thirty-one weeks pregnant. I was so scared. They gave me a shot twice. It was a steroid that helped to develop the baby's lungs, just in case I went into labour soon.

I was placed on strict bed rest. I couldn't do anything. Diary, it's interesting that we start to think about life and the things we can and can't do when someone decides to put rules on it. That was not happening for me. I refused to be on bed rest. While I was in the hospital,

I tried crawling to the patient kitchen. I even got my fiancé to get me a wheel chair just to wheel me around the hospital. Do you think I got away with that shit? Hell no. I got yelled at by my nurse, but she was nice. There was one day that I was craving chocolate, and she saw me trying to crawl on the floor to get it from the store inside the hospital. She went and bought it for me. I was so thankful. She told me that her thanks would be my staying inside my bed until my doctor gives me the clearance to go home. I eventually listened to her. After all, she did buy me my favourite chocolate—Ferrero Rocher. My doctor came at the end of the week and saw me.

The first thing that he asked me, as soon as I saw him, was, "Do you want to go home?" I said, "Yes, I do, and right now." He discharged me the next morning, on bed rest, though. Diary, I did not listen to that shit at all. I went to a walk-in clinic and got a note that said I was okay to go back to work. I just told the doctor that my feet were swollen, and that I had been resting for a week. He wrote the note, and I went right back to work. My coworkers knew exactly what I had done, because a couple of them had visited me in the hospital. They made sure that I didn't do the same work I did before getting admitted to the hospital. I was just praying to God to make it to winter break. That year, the last day of school before the holiday break was December 18th. I passed that day. Now, Diary, I was just hoping that I wouldn't give birth on Christmas Day. I was praying hard. I kept telling myself, *"I have a lot of food to eat on Christmas, and places to visit."* I told my stomach that it needed to behave until then. Christmas Day came, and I went to my soon-to-be mother-in-law's house, my mom's house, and my father's house that day.

When I went to my dad's house, I said, "I am going into labour tonight. I feel it." Nobody believed me. They were laughing at me, telling me to go relax. I just looked at them and shook my head. I asked my brother what time he wanted to head over to our mom's house, because remember, my parents are divorced, so we make double the trips on Christmas. Hey, I didn't mind at all, because double the trips meant double the food. My fiancé and I spoke throughout the day. We weren't on the best of terms, but we still expressed our love for each other. When we got to my mom's house, there were many jokes and lots of laughter, because all my brothers and sisters-in-law had different personalities, and it worked for us, most of the time. My stepdad had this tradition that every family dinner, and I mean every family dinner, we all went around in a circle and talked about what each of our kids has been up to, major achievements, and upcoming plans for each of us. That was always long, but it was also funny to see each of us on the spot, and we'd better say everything. If somebody knew something that you hadn't mentioned, they would call you out on it, so you had no choice but to share it. Around eleven in the night or so, I got the worst contraction I have ever felt in my life. I had to sit down on a chair and just breathe, while tears flowed down my face. My brother kept trying to talk to me, to see if I was okay, but I didn't answer him at all. His wife understood what I was going through and told my brother to just leave me alone until I was able to talk. Once I was okay, my family immediately jumped on me, asking me a thousand and one questions.

ADDITION

They asked me if I wanted to go to the hospital, if I wanted them to call my fiancé, if I wanted a drive home, and the list goes on. I told all of them to shut up, and that I was going home to go to sleep. I took my son home with me. Yes, Diary, I drove my ass home, and they were so worried about me. I told my mom that I would call her as soon as I got home. I put my son to bed, and then I went straight to sleep. Around two in the morning, I opened my eyes, and I said to myself that I needed to pee. The moment I stood up, my water broke. The first thing I did was call my dad to come get my son. My dad asked me why I hadn't called my fiancé yet, and rushed me off the phone to call him. I started laughing. My fiancé was at a holiday party when I called him. He sounded excited and nervous when I called. The next call I made was to the ambulance. I was having small contractions, but they were close together at that point. The operator on the phone was funny. He said, "Get a towel, a bowl of water, and a string." I had to ask him for what. He said, "I am preparing you to give birth at your house." I started laughing at him. I said, "No, you are not.

The ambulance better hurry up and get here. I will be having my baby in the hospital, thank you very much." He started laughing and told me that I made his night. He asked me, since I wasn't going to gather the items, to just make sure my door was unlocked and to sit on the floor. I could agree to that. As long as I had my baby at the hospital, I was good. He started laughing again, and he said I was the funniest person he had spoken to that had called emergency services while in labour.

The ambulance got there, and my fiancé arrived right as we were leaving. He took my son from the paramedic, and dropped him off to my dad before joining me at the hospital. Our son was born December 26, 2014. We were both so happy. My fiancé kept saying, "Thank you" to me, over and over and over again. It was kind of cute. Things were okay, but you would think things would've been better for a lot longer this time, seeing as we had just had a baby. He wasn't there the first night after our son was born, because he didn't make the necessary arrangements for his other kids. I won't even pretend to be okay with this. I was very upset about it. He even took three weeks off from work to spend time with me after I had the baby. Due to our arguing, he only came to see his son a couple times before returning to work.

I was done in my head, but not in my heart. The same shit kept happening with women. Secretly, I think the whole wedding invitation thing was my breaking point. That was when I felt as if I wasn't worth anything to him anymore. Clearly, he had doubts. Clearly, he had speculations. And now, to me, clearly, he didn't love me. You better believe we argued. I had to stand up for myself, and my love for him, and what he was pretending to show me. I had to call him out on it. I began to hate him inside. Well, at least, that's what I thought I began to feel. I didn't do anything like before when he had caught the guy at my house. But I did begin to feel as though I was becoming depressed, again. I was questioning myself whether I was even a good woman. I would talk to myself in my mirror and ask myself if I was pretty enough for him. Had I done enough for him? Was I being too hard on him? I asked myself a series of questions. I came up with all the answers, Diary, but they didn't match my actions. I told myself that he didn't truly love me, but I still ended up staying with him. I told myself that I wasn't pretty enough for him, but I still ended up smiling on his arm every time we went out. I lost myself in loving this man. I needed myself back. I didn't want to be like this anymore.

That is when I realized I had a pride issue, and no, I wasn't ready to deal with it. I didn't want to leave him and allow another woman to be with him, after all the work I had put in with him and for him. I refused to let another woman reap the benefits of my work. I would flip out. I couldn't even picture him with another woman, and I didn't want to picture him with somebody else. So yes, I stayed and I was proud of it. Nobody was going to steal my glory after everything I had done. No, no, no, no, you definitely got the wrong woman fucked up.

Diary, if I write this one more time, I know you're going to slap me, but I have to, because I am just keeping it real with you. Nothing changed. We would be good for a week, then argue for a week and a half, then he would disappear for a few days. It was our routine now. I could tell you what was going to happen like clockwork. That would've been a good thing if I were a boss, trying to help someone to get a job, but not in this case. It was getting really annoying to me, and I know it is getting annoying to you.

I started to not give a fuck about what I did or whom I talked to. My loyalty to him drifted away. I had people all around me telling me to leave this man, but I didn't. I refused to. So I strayed once again, but not to the extent I did the last time. Not to say it still isn't bad, but I felt as if I was careful this time. It's really not funny. I began talking to one of my exes—the one from my "surprise" birthday party situation. We spoke about what happened on my birthday. He said he had nothing to do with that, and doesn't speak to the guys that were involved anymore. I felt okay about that. We spoke more about life, and how things could be different. He told me that he loved me and wanted to see me again. I knew that I had to be careful and cautious. I told him about the guy that I was seeing, and that things were really rocky and not going as planned. I also told him that I had stopped caring. Diary, I even went as far as telling him that I didn't feel as if I was his woman anymore. He asked me if I wanted to come see him. I told him "yes," but I didn't go anywhere. We continued talking by text for a couple of days.

I would ask him if he had eaten, and if he hadn't, I would offer to bring him lunch. I told him I would, but I never did. There was always some excuse that I gave him, or I turned off my phone and then told him a story later on in the day when he messaged me again. I guess, subconsciously, I knew that what I was doing was wrong, and I was scared of what would happen if my fiancé found out. I wasn't trying to have a black eye again, or fight him in any way. As I said, it seemed as though the only time my fiancé and I knew how to communicate was when shit hit the fan, and this time was no different. It was only worse. We had been getting into arguments—the usual stuff about women, inconsistency, and other shit. He went through my phone and saw the messages that I was sending to my ex. He got mad and asked to talk. We went to my balcony to speak and try to reason. He was on one side of the balcony, and I was on the other. At this time, I felt inside myself that I didn't care if our relationship ended. He began telling me how he felt, and that he was sorry and still wanted us. Basically the same bullshit that I heard on a regular basis after he and I argued. When it was my turn to talk to him, I didn't say much.

I said something along the lines of "I don't care." I then looked at him and said, "This conversation is done," and I attempted to walk away and go back inside. That's when things turned ugly, within a millisecond. He immediately got up and pulled me by my hair, stating that he was going to throw me over the balcony. Clearly, he didn't, because I am here telling you about the incident. I lived on the eighth floor. I yelled out to him, "You're hurting me!" And he let go of my hair. He then did the same thing—he went outside and began crying. I went to my room and tried to go back to sleep, completely ignoring him for the rest of the night. He brought a chair into my room and sat down beside my bed, asking to talk to me. I didn't speak to him, but I did turn my body to hear what he had to say.

He apologized, again and asked me if he changed, if I would let go of my ex. He stayed at my house that night, and just watched over me. He took my phone and messaged my ex, telling him to stay away from me and that he was my fiancé. I don't know what the hell is wrong with me, but I felt kind of special. It felt as if he was fighting for me. I believed he wanted us. Everything was good for awhile, but the day after that night, I was not okay for a couple days. I had gone to work and basically cried the entire day. My co-workers asked me what was wrong, but I didn't say anything until later on in the afternoon. I guess I couldn't take it anymore. I wrote a note to my co-worker, telling her what had happened. I was telling her as a friend, not as a co-worker. She wrote back to me, saying that she had to tell the principal of my school. She told me that she was concerned about me and the kids. I begged her not to say anything, but she did. Another one of my co-workers was the lead hand in the special education area that I worked in. She told her first. I had left work at this point. They then went to the principal, who then had to call the police and make a report. Everything was okay for the rest of the day. I went to bed that night. Then around one in the morning, I awoke to a knocking at my door. It was the police, and they said some weird shit.

They said something about my son, and mentioned a school, but not the school he went to. I was very concerned. I stood at the door and spoke to them in my tank top and underwear. I was half asleep. They then told me that they were just doing a check-up call to make sure I was okay, because they had gotten third-party information. I told them that I didn't know what they were talking about, and that everything was fine. I even offered for them to come in and take a look. They declined and said that if anything was wrong, I shouldn't hesitate to call them. After I shut my door, I realized that they probably said what they did about my son to see if my fiancé was at the house or not, or if something was going on currently. I think they were ready to arrest him that night. But I felt I needed to protect him. That was the man I was going to marry, Diary. I couldn't sink him like that. A part of me was getting frustrated and concerned. I was thinking, *"This shit has gone too far now. What else is really going to happen? Is one of us going to lose our life over loving each other? Was this love, or was this possession?"*

He had placed his hands on me, again. He did the crying thing again, and he apologized again. Was this a pattern? Was this an honest mistake on his part? I don't know, but I began to realize that I had to do something, and I needed to do it fast if I really wanted to make our relationship better. The only problem was that I had felt for the longest time that I was doing this on my own. I felt as if I was fighting for us by myself. I brought up the idea of counselling to him, and he liked it and agreed. We spoke about communication between us, and said we needed to change things in our relationship on both ends. Remember, Diary, it takes two to tango, it takes two to talk, and it takes two to be in a relationship. We continued to have our ups and downs, but things never got physical between us for a very long time, which was good. We really needed to focus on our family before things got a lot worse. I began stressing, and weird stuff started happening to my body. I started getting these weird feelings in my head. I felt as though if I didn't stop moving my head really fast, my body would shut down. Was I going through postpartum depression? I really didn't think that at all. My fiancé thought that, because we kept arguing. Maybe he just needed to step up and be the man that I knew he could be. Our new son, our family, and I deserved his love as well. I went to the doctor, and the doctor placed me on a heart monitor for forty-eight hours. That's when I found out I was having heart palpitations.

I didn't have a clue what that was, but my doctor said that stress could cause it. Diary, are you trying to fucking tell me that this man was literally killing me inside out, and that he didn't even see it? Here is the thing: Shit didn't stop there. I started getting nightmares, a lot of them, and consistently. The nightmares weren't about anything that my fiancé and I were going through. They were about my uncle, the one that molested me. I would get dreams of him on top of me, grinding his body against mine, always touching me. I would wake up and go back to sleep, hoping the dream would change or just stop, but that didn't happen at all. The dream would just continue. It was as if that piece of dog shit was haunting me from afar. I started to believe that he had won. To me, he had won, because my mind couldn't get past this shit. My heart was still hurting from all the pain I had been through in my life, and I didn't feel as if I had anyone to talk to about it, without hearing the words "Get over it."

LISTEN

It was scary, and it left me feeling very stressed out. I had several panic attacks, and I knew I had to do something about it. I spoke to my old probation officer and my brother, and said that I wanted to charge my uncle. But what would that really do for me? Both my probation officer and my brother said "no," because they thought that that would just make things worse for me. And they were probably right, but I had to do something. I didn't want this to take over my life. I went back to my family doctor, told him how I was feeling, and he referred me to a psychiatrist. In the meantime, while waiting for the psychiatrist, I went to see a counsellor. I didn't have to pay for anything. I signed up through my workplace. She was okay, I guess, but what she suggested to me didn't work at all. She told me to try and change my mind. If I woke up from a nightmare, I should walk around for a bit, then get a pen and paper and write a different ending to the story. I thought that maybe this would work, but it fucking didn't. Some nights, it made it worse. It was like my mind was battling itself. I felt as if my mind got mad at me for trying to write a different ending. So when I went back to sleep, the nightmare felt even more real, like I was still living it. Diary, how could I really write a different ending to the story, when my mind and my heart already knew the truth? My mind knows what happened. I can't just erase that. I finally got the call from the hospital to see the psychiatrist. I went for a psychiatric assessment. The doctor I saw seemed really nice and concerned.

She asked me a whole lot of questions, and came closer to me at certain parts, and then became distant at others. I think she was trying to see my reaction. She told me that she saw a lot of anxiety in me, and saw that I needed some type of therapy and counselling. She suggested that I sign up for DBT therapy, which stands for Dialectic Behavioural Therapy. This was used for people who had anxiety and PTSD (Post-Traumatic Stress Disorder). I was diagnosed with three things: Anxiety, PTSD, and Borderline Personality Disorder. This was a lot to take in, but it was a start. She told me to tell my family doctor to re-refer me in the springtime, due to a backlog of patients at the hospital where I would receive counselling. She placed me on three different medications—one for anxiety, one for sleep, and the last one was for nightmares. I was very apprehensive about taking them, and the psychiatrist could see that.

She told me to take them on a weekend, to see how my body would adjust to them, because I told her about my weekly schedule.

Before I left her office, she spoke to me about some tricks to try to help with the anxiety and nightmares. She said she was going to send the information to my family doctor and give recommendations of any possible medication changes, just in case any problems arose. I was feeling good about beginning to take back my life, but I was scared because I didn't want my family to think I was crazy. I told my brother, mom, and dad about it. They were all hesitant but supportive. My brother thought that I had to also change my diet and the way I slept at night. He told me that whenever he slept on his left side, he always had nightmares and cold sweats. I did know that I needed to change my eating habits, but I knew my eating habits had absolutely nothing to do with the way I was feeling and what I was going through with my nightmares. But, Diary, did you know that your diet can affect the way you sleep at night? I did not know that. I told my fiancé about this, and he was extremely supportive and proud of me. He also reiterated that he thought I was suffering from postpartum depression, which I highly disagreed with, but I didn't have the energy to debate that with him. He said that he would come to counselling sessions with me, and even get marriage counselling for both of us.

I wanted to tell him that I thought he also needed individual counselling to help him properly grieve and move on from things in his life, but that was a whole different battle that, I am sorry to say, I was not willing to have. This may seem selfish, but I needed to focus on myself, and if that meant leaving him behind, then I guess that's what I had to do. I was trying to understand the way my body reacted, along with my mind and heart, when it came to our relationship. We didn't argue as much anymore, but that wasn't necessarily a good thing. We weren't arguing much because we stopped communicating with each other. I would stop talking to him for a couple days, and then send a random message saying that I loved him, and I'd ask him if he wanted to come with me to pick up our son from daycare. There were times when I wouldn't respond to any of his messages, and I'd make it known that I had read them. He would write stuff like "I love you," "You mean the world to me," "I don't want to lose us," and so on. Things got really bad, but whatever.

We set a date for our son's christening, which was January 17, 2016. We spoke about doing separate christenings, because he said that he didn't want to fake his feelings. Don't worry, we didn't do that. I think we were both just being selfish, even bringing up that idea to try and hurt each other. We stayed together, and we had the christening together. It was good. His friends and family came. We got into a slight argument that day because of his family members who came to the church and refused to wait for him, so that irritated him a bit, and he always took his emotions out on me. So obviously, I got the attitude from him. I get it, though, I guess. Diary, I think you should just have a page of sayings, because I am about to tell you another one. There is a saying that when we are upset, we tend to take it out on the people who are the closest to us, which is not right in any way. Moving on from that slight hurdle in the day, the reception was at my mom's house, and it was a good thing that I had the key to her house from before, so it made it a lot easier to have everything clean and prepared before that day.

We had fun at my mom's house. The kids played, we said a prayer, and my fiancé and I got along just fine. That night, we had the most amazing make-up sex ever. Again, I feel as though I am repeating myself, over and over. Everything was all good for a couple of weeks, and then we were back to the same old back-and-forth arguments. These weren't just simple arguments anymore. They started to become very disrespectful on both parts. It was like a game of who could hurt who more. When you're connected to someone, actions aren't the only things that hurt, our words can hurt, too, and sometimes even more. I called him a deadbeat father, and he called me a cemetery. I used to feel protected by this man, but now I felt as if he had stopped protecting me and had begun protecting someone else. It was weird. He stopped calling me by name. Sometimes he would call me "Chris," which he never used to do before. I knew in my head that he was talking to someone else, but I never voiced it, because I didn't have solid proof. We grew more distant from each other as each day passed by.

He definitely stopped caring, and so did I. We were still together. I don't understand why we didn't just call it quits. Was it control on both of our ends? I don't know, but it was bad and very unhealthy. I wasn't happy, and he clearly wasn't either. He completely stopped coming to see our son. The only time he would see him was if I reached out to him and asked him to come with me to pick up the children. I knew now in my heart that he was seeing somebody else, but I still didn't have the proof, and to be honest, I didn't really care to hurt my brain over it. We would argue, but I stopped answering his messages and calls, because I got tired of hearing the same shit. It wasn't going to change, and I was not going to try to change him at all. I began talking to a guy from my past. He messaged me on Facebook, but I didn't answer right away. As things became more distant between us, to the point where I even told him I didn't want him anymore, I became more interested in responding to this other guy. It got to the point where I said, "It's over. I don't love you. I don't want you. Leave me alone." So I tried to move on with my life, and I replied to the guy on Facebook.

He would message me every day, check up on me, ask me how my kids were, and always make time for me. I felt loved as a person, and the best thing of all was that I didn't need to get to know him from scratch, because I already knew him. It was all about catching up on life with each other now. The reason I say that is because I'd always said if things didn't work out with my fiancé, I would refuse to talk to another guy. I didn't want to get to know or understand another man's life story. This was more like continuing a chapter that was closed a very, very long time ago. He had some issues with the mother of his children, but he told me that they were no longer together. What made me fall for him, though, was his passion for God and his determination to make it in life. He told me about the Bible, and we would pray together. He educated me on the background of holidays like Easter, and what it really meant. We finally got to see each other. I went out to eat with my friends at a restaurant, and I told him that he could meet us there to grab something to eat. He came, and when I hugged him, I felt warm and beautiful. I was happy to see him.

My fiancé and I were in my car back in February of 2016, and we got into an accident in a parking lot, and the front end of my car was damaged. My insurance company refused to fix it, because I wasn't the person driving my vehicle. I explained the situation to the guy I had started talking to again, and he asked to see the car. I showed him, and he fixed it temporarily. He popped the dent out, and put the cap back on over the fog light. It didn't look bad at all. It looked a lot better. I gave him a hug and a kiss for helping me. I began to miss him when we parted ways. I had the feeling, very deep down, that maybe this wasn't completely right, but I didn't feel as if I was doing anything wrong on the surface, because my now ex-fiancé and I didn't talk at all. I interpreted it as meaning we weren't together. I told my fiancé that we weren't together, so why did I feel like talking to someone else was wrong, deep down? Maybe it was because I still had feelings for him. I don't know, but I knew that even if this connection was temporary, I felt really good inside.

NO

Then on the night of March 20, 2016, my fiancé—I don't even know why I am still calling him that at this point—called me, and we got into a really big argument. I blamed him for our entire relationship. I told him that if he was half the man that he said he was, we wouldn't have been in the mess that we were in now. I told him that I was interested in somebody else, and that I was talking to that person, but I didn't tell him that we had seen each other. He was thrown off by what I said, and didn't believe me at all. About twenty minutes later, I got a phone call from him saying, "Yeah, you have a new man? Well, here is your man's first test: Go fix your car." I got really worried about what he had said about my car. This was around half-past ten at night. I called one of my really close friends, and I told her to stay on the phone with me while I went to check on my car. I told her what he had said to me, and she was very concerned, but we tried to laugh it off. When I went downstairs to my car, I didn't know that my life was about to change so drastically and fast, all in that one night.

"I Still Love You"

It's been eight-and-a-half years now, and we still ain't married. Don't you think I'm worth it after all your babies I carried? Our oldest son is in the grave, and yes, my heart still blames you for your selfish ways. I don't think you understand how much you have hurt me, but yet you take pride in telling me women want to be me. Sometimes I wondered if you even wanted to see me. You have all these girls on the side, but you call me your superstar. You thought I would always ride. You cheated on me with one of your kids' mothers, having her tell me that he could even have a brother. We were engaged, we even had a baby on the way, and somehow you still convinced me that it was all okay. You hid behind my back to sneak a friendship with a girl you would always call "wack." I was at my breaking point then. I knew I wanted to do something, but I just didn't know when. She even put you in jail, taking you away from me, but somehow, again, you were okay with the things she would say to me. I felt as if she was always in your front seat, and when you needed me, then you'd look back for me. You knew she still wanted you, so you used her against me, showing me you would gladly replace me. I put all that aside, because when I looked in your eyes, it's crazy, I still saw that I was your wife. In that same year, in mid-November, we found out you'd be going to jail, and yes, it left my heart tender. On weekends, you wouldn't be with me. I was at your mother's house. Trust me, we both anticipated your collect call. When your weekends ended, it seemed everything changed. You claimed you loved me, but all I felt was pain. We would argue all the time. I felt distance. When I would say, "I love you," all you would do was show a lot of resistance. I would call you on your way to work, and you would brush me off, saying you were listening to music. In my mind, I was going crazy. I thought I was going to lose it. I became distant, and started playing your game. I wondered if you would think the actions were okay. But you didn't. You caught him coming to my door, and my heart was trying to even your score. I was looking for love, for someone to talk to, but every time I linked you, it was like you were telling me, "Let go." You didn't need me anymore. How did you feel when you caught him at my door? I lied to you and told you he was my cousin. After you called, my mind started bugging. I knew what you wanted to do that night; you could've kill him, maybe me too, but you know that ain't right. We were trying to work it out, but both of us had doubts. You saw a text, and you saw all my doubts. You punched me in my face, leaving my eye looking like a 2003 blackout. You then started crying. I held you. I forgave you. Only then you started trying. You were the husband I had always wanted, my best friend, my everything. I never questioned *why you gave me a ring. Things were good for about two months. After that, it was like kicking you in and out of the house. You became that jerk again, entertaining girls. You were working hard for them. I questioned how many of them showed you their pearls. You would deny me in front of the world. We continued to have our ups and downs. Then in 2014, it was about time we settled down. We were going to Jamaica. I was going to be your wife, the one that would die by your side. I even bought the invitations, and we were ready to hand them out. But you lied to me and gave me a cop-out. I still stayed. My heart was frail, and I was afraid. I didn't want to lose you, but it seemed I was playing number two. I could go on to all the ways that you've done me wrong, but I still want us. We used to be that power couple that was all about trust. It got to the point where the distance was more than strong. It was like the devil, but this time he won. March 21st happened, and it tore us apart. It seemed as if we were living in the dark. The system was now against us. You got bail, but was there any hope for us? We came back together, and that is when I realized we could get through the darkest weather.*

November 28th was the trial date. They want me to testify. I am going to lie for you, but don't think that means your actions are justified. I want to put this all behind us and focus on our family and the values in life. I still want to *be your wife. I'll marry you and give you my life. I need your help! I don't want to do this on my own. You're my kind, so sit proudly on that thrown. I am your queen; don't place me as anything less, because I'm supposed to be your right hand and your best friend. Start helping me pay the bills and take care of the kids. I know you work hard, but we still need to live. You're my hero, my king, and my everything. I'll meet you down the aisle so that we can consolidate things. I'll proudly carry your name. You and I have a ten-year-old that will do the same. I'll bear another child for you. I hope it will be a girl, so we can spoil her and teach her about the world. We need to show our kids what true love is. You're my best friend in the world. Baby, don't worry, I'm still proud to be your girl. Let's come together and unite. God is our third strand, so let's give him our hands. I can go on forever about our love story, but make sure in the end you're my man, and I'll always be your shorty.*

Diary, I just needed to get that off my chest before I tell you what happened that night on March 21st. That made it a lot easier for me, Diary. My heart hurts about that night, and it's not even just about the pain that he and I were in. It was the damage that we both caused to, and within, our families. Here I go. I went downstairs to the underground parking to see my car. I just had to make sure that my car was okay. I looked around, and I didn't see him, and my car was okay. I then went and pressed the button to the elevator to go back upstairs, and that's when he stormed through the other door that was in my building, in case you wanted to take the stairs instead of the elevator. He fought me for my keys and cell phone. My friend was screaming on the phone, telling both of us to stop and calm down. He ripped my sweater down by the zipper and got my keys and phone. I followed him throughout the underground parking, screaming at him and trying to fight him for my stuff. I yelled to him that the kids were upstairs, so he took my house keys and threw them towards me. I looked for them on the ground before heading back upstairs. When I got upstairs, he was there. I opened my door, and he grabbed me by my neck and pushed me inside.

I tripped over the shoes at the door, hitting my head as I fell and landed on my left hand. He stood over me. He wanted to kick me, but he didn't. He walked over me and said he wanted to kill me. The phone started ringing. It was a random number. I had screamed to my friend on the phone to call the police while we were fighting in the underground. So I guess she did. I asked him to give me the phone so I could answer it, just in case it was the police calling to see if I was okay. He refused to give me back my phone. He answered then hung up. I'll explain to you why he didn't want to give me back my phone. He was probably hoping that the guy would call so he could answer. I was thanking God that he didn't call. He left my house with my keys and my phone. Shortly after, he knocked on my door again, but I was crying and refused to open the door, so he left.

My friends came creeping down the hallway. Now I can laugh, but if you saw them, it was really funny. They were tiptoeing to the door like Shaggy and Scooby Doo. I immediately began crying in their arms. They knew I was hurt. I was crying and telling them to call the guy I was talking to, because I was worried about what would happen if my fiancée got a hold of him on the phone. Everything came crashing down in my world. It was so surreal to me. They called my dad, brother, and emergency services back. My blood pressure was really high, and my blood sugar was low. When the paramedic was asking me questions, I could hear my dad asking my friends questions. I immediately started crying and screaming to not let him through the door. I knew he just wanted to protect me, but I didn't want anything worse to happen. The police calmed my dad down in my house.

EYES

❦

I knew my ex-fiancé was still around. I knew he never left. He's the type of person that wants to see who comes around. He was probably waiting around to see if I had called the guy over to help me. I was getting ready to go on the stretcher. My dad was talking to me, but I can't even remember what he was saying. I couldn't stop thinking about what had just happened, and what was about to happen and change because of everything that was happening right now. I did not want to be alive. I wanted to turn back the hands of time, and just forget everything and everyone. All I remember is that he said, "Your brother is on his way to the hospital," and that he would meet me there. While we were going to the elevator, I heard the dispatcher over the police walkie talkie saying that they had apprehended him. I immediately started crying, but I was also very angry with him. The police woman said it didn't matter if I didn't want to press charges, because they were going to press charges against him, just based on what my friend had said and heard from the fight on the phone. I was like, *"Oh, fuck,"* in my head. I actually felt really bad that he was arrested.

Before the ambulance drove off, a police officer came to the back of the ambulance and gave me back my phone and keys.

I felt it was over in my head. I already told you, Diary, I could feel in my heart that he was seeing somebody else, and I found out the next day who that somebody else was. When he got out of jail, he posted a picture of a woman with his mother, with the caption underneath saying, "Then I met you." I knew he had posted that purposely, just so I would see it. So I unblocked him to let him know that I had seen it. It was only that one day that we expressed animosity or anger towards each other. He wasn't allowed to talk to me directly. We began communicating through statuses, and we both expressed that we loved and missed each other. It was cute, I guess. It was just a fucked-up situation that we both regretted. Everyone around us had been affected, but nobody was more affected than our children, and we both knew that somehow, someway, we had to fix this. Even if we didn't get back together, it needed to be fixed, so that the kids wouldn't get affected, and if they did, that the effect would be very minimal.

I did get mad at first, because I was thinking, "*This man fought me for my phone and my keys because I said that*

I was interested in someone else, but he had somebody else on the side the entire time." When I realized who the woman was, I just laughed with anger, because there was a time when he and I had argued about her. A week went by, and that's when I finally became brave enough to actually call him. He never said a word to me the entire time, except for when I said "I love you." He responded by saying that he still loved me, too. We began talking more indirectly through statuses. Then on April 9th, Diary, he came back to me. We spoke. I held him. I touched him and kissed him. I knew he knew that I missed him. I sat on the couch with him for a bit. He was speechless. He was really hurt, especially by the fact that our son woke up, and it was as if he had forgotten who his dad was. He hadn't seen him for weeks, and he was just a baby.

I put our son back down before going back to the couch to talk to him. I began crying on his shoulder, and I knew he didn't like to see or hear me cry. The moment he felt my tear drop on him, he began holding me tightly, and we made love that night. It was amazing, but we knew that the road in front of us was far from over. We agreed to get the others out of our lives and focus on us. It took him longer than it took me, but he did it. He then confessed to me that he had slept with the girl and had taken her out on her birthday, after we were back together. It hurt, but I was just focused on us getting our family back. I still had a lot of anger, and I know he did too, so I tried to understand where he was coming from. In his eyes, I had put him in jail to be with another man, when, in fact, it had nothing to do with another man. After the whole balcony situation that I told you about, he told me that if he ever put his hands on me again, I should put him in jail. Diary, since we were so distant for so long, and it wasn't getting any better, only worse, I felt no way about putting him in jail. I was tired of the shit, and I needed him to know that.

His main thing was that he couldn't believe that I had made a statement against him. I tried to explain to him that this wasn't the first time that he had done it, and yes, I was angry, but more importantly, I was afraid that if I told the police that nothing happened, that my children could possibly have been in jeopardy. He tried to understand my point of view, but I guess things were so fresh that anger took over for both him and me. We continued arguing for months after that day about who was more wrong than the other person, who cheated on who, who needed to put more work in, all types of shit. It was annoying, and a part of me wanted to give up, again, but then I said to myself that I knew that I wasn't going anywhere. My co-worker introduced to me to a particular movie, because she saw me writing down a prayer, so she thought I had watched it, but I hadn't. I watched the trailer for the movie on my phone. It was really good. It was good to the point where I went out and actually paid full price for the movie. Diary, I did not want a bootleg copy of it; it looked that good. He came over that night, and we watched it together. We both cried at certain parts. It brought us together that night for a little bit. After a couple days, we began arguing again.

I think we really needed to stop and ask ourselves, "Why are we arguing with each other? What is hurting us the most? We know we love each other, but why can't we just seem to get it right?" It took me awhile to actually get it, to be honest. Diary, I started falling victim to what the social media outlets have pushed upon us these days about how a man is supposed to treat a woman. Don't get me wrong, I expect my soon-to-be husband to have respect for me, to value me, to treat me right, and to love me. However, we were both going about it the wrong way. One day I watched the movie again and again and again, and I cried each time I watched it. I needed a voice of reason. I needed a voice of real power. And I needed my voice back. My fiancé was not my enemy; he was supposed to be my strength, lover, best friend, and companion. It was time for me to take my life back. It was time for me to rise above my past and make it the reason for my success. Diary, it was time for me to face my battles with resources and positive people. It was time for me to be my own voice, and the voice of others who feel silenced. It was time for me to be happy. It was time for me to be the real me, Diary.

A Letter to an Evolving Woman;

You got love ambassadors telling you what to expect from a man, but what can you expect from a man when you can't even look in the mirror proudly and say, "I know who I am." A lot of women are looking for love in the wrong places, wearing tons of make-up, you can't even see their true face. The media will have your mind confused; listen to your heart sometimes, it knows the truth. More women need to elevate one another on their successes. We need to stand together and show them what one is. Especially Black women, why are we always trying to bring one another down? Don't you know the others look at us like clowns? Why can't we educate each other, and love one another? Aren't you tired of fighting over a man? Let's help each other get jobs and scream like Nas the rapper, "I know I can!" Education is key, and self-worth is a need. Stop being the woman who can't stand on her own two feet.

Don't let a man guide you before finding out his truth and attributes. God has to be the one who sent him to protect you. A lot of women think they need a man in their life. Open your eyes, many of you are still alone at night. You need yourself and your pride. Stop hiding behind a mask that you didn't buy. You need to understand yourself, your love, your worth, and then try. Don't give up just because you didn't succeed. It's okay to cry, and it's even okay to bleed. Set your dreams high, and work hard for them. Nobody can bring you down, especially when you're used to them. Open your eyes and build your empire. Stop finding devils; they are only liars. Be a virtuous woman, and set goals for yourself. You can't love a man when you don't love yourself. Some women have men in their lives and another man on the side. It's sad, especially when a baby is caught in a lie. Women have given a new meaning to the word "submissive," but unyielding is really what your truth is. It's not good to have men in and out of your life; your body needs to be your highest prize. Not everyone should have your body; you're a queen. Narrow-minded people will think that what I'm saying is targeting and mean. Sometimes we women are the problem, and we look to our men, hoping they'll solve them. I see a lot of quotes of men doing wrong. Well, I'll be the first woman to tell you that not all men are truly wrong. How can you expect your man to choose only you, but laugh at him because he's still taking the bus? We need to help our men, if we want their help, too. Don't be the woman who thinks she's too good to even have a man look at her. We need to humble ourselves and come together as a team. We need to stand as women and state what we mean. Stop letting others tell us and show us what they think we are. We all have our stories about how strong we are. I am not here to try and bring us down. I'm just here to state facts, so we know what to do. I am a woman, too. I'll always stand with you, but we can't say we'll ride or die, if our story is full of hidden lies. Let's get to the root of our problems, so we can solve them. Then we can all stand together as one and show them what real woman are, and what we can become.

HEAL

༺☙❧༻

Diary, I don't understand why so many people fall victim to false outlets, like social media apps and videos. I was one of them. Even the news outlet was terrible. They share the portion of the story that's the catchiest, without stating all the facts, leaving viewers like us with false judgements. It's just disgusting, and I am happy that I have woken from the dark clouds and realized that happiness comes from myself. Values come from your upbringing and practices. Happiness doesn't come from people in your life. They are just supposed to add to your life, but not complete it. I am happy, Diary, that I finally decided to take action, and this is how I started, Diary.

I hope you're proud of me, or starting to be. I know a lot of these pages were written with a lot of negativity, but they shaped and moulded me into the woman I am today, and am still becoming. My firstborn is the one who started to change me for the better. I even got a tattoo that says, "Because of you, I am no longer a prisoner," with his name and date of birth. There was no way that I wanted him to grow up and tell me that he is a drug dealer, or is disrespectful to women, or is caught up in the streets with negative women and men. I began to try and better myself, and it started while I was in the residence for young mothers. My primary worker and my probation officer pushed me hard throughout my stay, and never settled for less from me. I always told my probation officer that I was going to go to college. Obviously, she had doubts about me doing that, but I had to prove everyone wrong, in a good way. And I definitely had to prove myself right. Diary, after I moved into my apartment in Scarborough, I immediately started looking up colleges.

I knew that I wanted to do something with kids, but just didn't know what. I looked into two programs: Nursing and Child and Youth Worker. I weighed out my options, and realized that I wanted to be a Child and Youth Worker, because there was more gain for me. I want to touch the lives of young men and women who are trying to turn their lives around for the better. Sometimes, all it takes is the right voice for someone to evolve and become who they are intended to be. I had to take a test, because I was applying as a mature student. Diary, I never finished high school, so applying as a mature student to a college meant I was over nineteen years of age, and I had to take a math and English test to determine my eligibility to get into the school. When I went to do the test, I was in a room with other people. It looked like a computer lab. The instructor gave us headphones. It was a multiple choice test.

I was very nervous while completing the test, and after I finished, I couldn't stop being anxious while waiting for my call back or email from them. Diary, YAY! That day of anxiety finally came to an end. I PASSED! I FUCKING PASSED! I was so excited. The day came when I had to go take my college identification photo. I was so happy. I immediately sent it to my mom, dad, and brother. They were so happy for me, but I knew deep down they were sceptical, except for my brother. I can't hide my feelings. I was scared for myself in college. I was scared that I was going to drop out. And every time I had doubts, I just looked at the photo of my son and remembered that I had to do it for him. I had so many dreams, and I wanted to achieve them. The work was pretty easy. It was just the amount of work that we got at one time. I understood very fast that the moment you get an assignment, start it, because it will all pile up and catch up on you quickly, and then that's when you'll feel as if you're drowning in school work.

As I already told you, I wanted to drop out of school in my second year. It was really hard for me that I didn't get to see my son throughout the week. I was doing placement from 7:30 am to 3:00 pm, or from 3:00 pm to 11:00 pm. It would alternate every week. The shit that would go down at placement sometimes, Diary, meant my ass wasn't leaving on time. Girls trying to fight staff, running away, or getting involved in escorting services. It was some scary shit sometimes, but I enjoyed it, because this was what I had a passion for. This was my career, and I had to be prepared for what came with it. Diary, there was one night that one of the girls that we suspected were involved in escorting wanted to get out, and she confided in a staff member. Her pimp was coming to pick her up, but she didn't want to go. The house started receiving threats of harm if we didn't allow her to go outside. He told us he would be coming back with a gun, if we didn't let her out within the next fifteen minutes.

We had a big staff meeting the next day, where the manager just went over safety tips with the staff, like walking in pairs, parking in a visible space, and so forth. It was worth it, though. The experience I got was amazing. I was happy with what I was doing and happy that my second year of college was almost over. I thought that my second year was rough for me, which it was, but my last year of college was a roller coaster, in my opinion. I had ups and downs with my fiancé throughout school, as you know, Diary, but that was the least of my problems. My schooling was jeopardized because I got into some problems with a stupid-ass bitch. Yes, Diary, I know I've changed, but I still didn't like the girl. Forgive me for my language. This girl and I ended up having the same placement together. She and I were the only ones on the same floor for placement, so I was her competition. She told the staff that I said some things about them, which caused a lot of tension on the floor when we were working. I didn't lose my placement. However, my placement coordinator and the one who hired me advised me to start over somewhere else, and that I was a strong person. The one who had hired me didn't want me to go, but wanted me to get the best education I could, because he saw the passion and drive in me.

Diary, I did just that and ended up with an A+. From what I heard about the girls, she put her own foot in her mouth for her placement. I can say one thing to that, Diary—Karma. I highly believe in it at all times. I heard from some people in my school that she had made a negative comment about my son, and that's when I was ready to flip. Diary, you better believe that I went looking for her in the school, and she found out I was looking for her and called her parents and the police. While I was in class, two security guards came for me to bring me downstairs. One of my classmates made a joke about the security guards, asking them if they wanted his help, because I could take on both of them. He was the class joker and a really good friend of mine to this day. When I got downstairs, there were two police officers in a backroom, and we spoke. They basically put me on some conditional foolishness with the security guards. I never got a charge, thank goodness. It was more or less saying that if this girl and I got into problems for the remainder of the school year, there would be an investigation, and I would be out of school.

That meant I wouldn't be able to graduate on time. Fucking hell, I was pissed off. All I said to the police officers was, "When people realize that you're bigger than them, they run, but when they see that they can bully you, they have a problem with it." The police understood where I was coming from when I told them that I wouldn't allow someone to disrespect my children. It was a tense few weeks after that, but I made it. I truly made it. I heard she was still talking her shit, and when I heard about it, yes, I did have to challenge myself mentally, because people like to stir up drama, so they could either be making it up or adding their own mix to what she actually said. I ended up going to our office in the school to speak to one of my teachers, and one of them stopped me in the hall—one I didn't like—and told me some bullshit. She basically told me some shit she would teach me in class. She wasn't real with me; it was as if she didn't care what I felt or anything.

DETERMINATION

☙❧

Diary, you want to hear the funniest thing ever? Exactly what I told you that I felt she was saying was exactly what it was. I went to class after, where I could speak to another teacher, and she kept it real with me. She gave me advice and inspiration, but when she started teaching the lesson, the same thing that the other teacher had told me was the same thing she was teaching. In my head, I said, *"This bitch."* But you know what? School was more than almost over for me, so I just had to keep my head in the game. I was finished school, Diary, and with a job already. My graduation was amazing. It felt so good to see the smiles on my parents' faces and my fiancé's face, and to receive good words from my probation officer and primary worker from Rosalie Hall as well as the people in my life. I felt really good.

Diary, this was a major step toward bettering myself and understanding who I truly am. A lot of people have told me that they don't understand how or why I am still alive, and that they would have killed themselves. But, Diary, what good would that really do? I want to become a motivational speaker as well as achieve my Child and Youth Worker career, and I am still looking for avenues to do so. I am not going to give up on my dreams. I promise you, Diary. I have come too far in my life for me to just fall asleep on myself. It was something that always ran through my mind, especially when I was watching those talk show hosts, and they would bring out the professionals to help straighten out the lives of the young ones. My favourite talk show back then was Maury. I would run home just to watch that show. I am very happy that I didn't succeed with my many suicide attempts, or I wouldn't be here to tell you about me, the real me, because whenever someone tries to tell you about someone else, they always leave out the truth behind the hidden lies. Suicide isn't a joke at all, and it's not something that should ever be taken lightly.

A lot of people say that people who have contemplated suicide, or have succeeded in doing it, are weak, but I feel in my heart that they are some of the strongest people that have walked among us. Do you know how amazing our body is? When a person wants to harm themselves, the body naturally stops them from doing so. The brain is an amazing thing. So for someone to actually come up with a plan that overcomes their body's resistance, it shows strength. I think that society, as a whole, needs to start addressing suicides with more awareness, compassion, and understanding. We spread awareness about gun violence and death. We need to start reaching out to people who are struggling with their mental health before they get to that point. As I tell you, Diary, the system is a big joke. They know exactly what they are doing. They don't want to help us. Remember, the more awareness and light we shed, the less need we will have for their big jobs. I'm not stupid. I caught on a long time ago. Only then will we be able to help those in need. People struggle with communication, and that is their way of asking for help. I am tired of people turning a blind eye to mental health. It's real, and a lot of cultures deny it. Mine is one of them, but I'll get to that later.

When I got hired to the TDSB, I was able to work a couple of shifts before summer, so I could have the experience of getting paid for the job that I have always wanted. During the summer, I was on welfare for the three years that I was in school. I used something called OSAP when I was in school. They helped with the costs of living and providing for my dependents, but in the summertime when school was finished, I had to maintain a source of income so that both my son and I were taken care of. After graduation, I was able to get a contract right away for the upcoming September. I was hired at Agincourt Collegiate Institute. I worked there for two years. During my time there, I ran across a lot of students that came from all walks of life. Some struggled with communication with their teachers, home life, street life, crime, and lack of knowledge. During my second year there, the principal asked me to run a girls group to help the at-risk young girls in the school who required assistance with their self-esteem, body image, home life, street life, and academics.

These girls were, and still are, very special to me. They are very unique in their own way, and all have their own stories. Some of their stories broke my heart. Sometimes principals, parents, and even the police had to get involved due to the nature of some of their situations. You would think that these girls wouldn't trust me, because I told them that, depending on what they told me, I had a legal obligation to report certain situations to my boss and the authorities. But it wasn't like that at all. They would hug me, cry in my arms, and say "thank you." It was moving and touching.

That's when I decided that I wanted to start a career in motivational speaking and uplifting young women and men. These girls became my "daughters." All of them have taken different paths. Some of them have left that school and have gone on to another to try and further their education, and some have stayed to try and stick it out. Diary, one thing I learned in my field was to leave work at work. When you get home, focus on home. I have engraved that in my mind; however, it's not engraved in my heart. I truly believe that when you have a passion for something, you should go hard for it. At any time, someone's life could come crashing down. Being someone's strength in their time of need does not require a time limit, but rather boundaries. You cannot put a limit on love and passion.

I then acquired a permanent position in the school board. I went back to my girls group at the high school on Tuesdays. However, that was easier said than done. Due to different work hours—high schools are usually let out earlier than elementary schools—and due to the high needs of the students at my new permanent position, I would often have to cancel the group. I was still able to set my expectations with the girls, and let them know what I expected of them. I think about them a lot, Diary, and, to be honest, I worry for a couple of them. I hope that they are able to find their voices, and find someone that they can trust to help them. I found that voice for myself, and luckily, it was more than one person. I hope that they are able to find love within themselves, trust within their hearts, compassion within their minds, and self-worth within their thoughts. Diary, I worked at other high schools and ran both young men's and young women's groups. I need a moment to pray for them, as I miss all of them dearly, and I hold them in high esteem in my life.

Dear my Agincourt Women, SATEC Men and Women, and Monarch Park C.I. Women and Men,

I know that you guys have been dealt a rough path, and I know that some of you are still struggling to find your way. I write this letter to you to read in silence, so that you can read and understand, then break your silence with strength. I have given you all my words of experience, compassion, and knowledge. I have suggested what to do in times of need and sorrow. I know that you guys will evolve into beautiful women and handsome men. Love yourself before you love someone else. You cannot fix yourself by breaking someone else down. I know that many of you believe that some of your teachers don't like you, and that may be true, but when you feel as if someone has done wrong to you, uplift them with kindness and respect. Your values are self-taught. Nobody can predict where you will end up in your life. Nobody chooses your dreams, except you. Whenever you have a nightmare, get up, and even though the ending does not change, you need to make your new ending. Your ending is success through strength and determination as you grow. Make your success your strongest weakness. When I say that, I mean your success must never be taken for granted, but it must always be protected, valued, and embraced. Anything can be taken from you at any given time, but when it comes to your self-worth, don't ever let anybody take that crown off your head. You are princesses and princes, developing into queens and kings. I love you all, and I am still cheering for you, and will never stop.

Love, Ms. Lewis, a.k.a Mom

Oh, Diary, you're so lucky you're not human. You don't have to go through struggles, but at the same time, I wonder if you feel my pain or hear my cries while I write to you at night. I wonder if you can understand and grasp a thought that I may have. I wonder all of these things. I don't want to take you for granted. I want you to know that I appreciate your dedication and commitment to me. I appreciate that you give me the chance to truly express myself, without judging me. I just wanted to say thank you. Some may find this weird, because you can't talk back, but I can hear you, especially when I reread what I've written. Sometimes I cry when I reread what I write to you, and other times I don't write what I really want to. I now know that everybody has at least one secret that they do not want to share with anyone, not even a diary, because there is a chance that the secret could come out and then the silence would have been broken without the strength being revealed. As I write, I like to self-reflect. Sometimes I doubt myself in being a positive voice for these young women and men because of the things that I have done or have been through. I realize that my doubt is my only weakness, and that it is my only enemy. I have to overcome my enemy.

When I feel and know that I am doing better and getting somewhere, I begin to doubt myself. I question if I can really do it. Even in writing this book, I have doubted myself, but it has only become my strength. You have to fight your fears with facts. You have to bring yourself positivity. Positive influence and positive self-awareness are important parts of life as well as the sense of self. I am happy that I have overcome the obstacles that many thought would break and kill me. I am happy that I have met positive people in the police force that others frown upon. There's good and bad in every field. I am happy I can say that I am not a product of my environment or circumstances. I am proud to be that voice, and now I need to become that image as well. I still have some personal struggles, but I have realized that if I really want to overcome them, then I first need to accept them, and then make a plan to rise above them.

Diary, I'm getting sad. I am running out of pages to write to you. I need to write down a special part before you run out of room for me to write. I don't even know whether to call it a letter or a piece. This is really hard for me. I guess I can say that this is a symbol of my love.

CHILDREN

When I first began to write my book, I didn't want my children to read it. Now that I have embraced this journey, I want them to fully embrace me. I can't hide what I am not ashamed of. My life and my past have moulded me into the mother that I have become for them. It has given me patience and values that I must teach them. They are my greatest accomplishment in life. I call my firstborn "My Child." He is my day one, the one who helped me in the most honest, realest, and most revealing way. Then I had my second son, whom I call "My Baby." My little light-skinned child, the one who keeps me on my toes, and has added to my family. I love you, my children. Mommy has to tell you sorry for a lot of things. I hope you two grow up to become strong, independent, God-serving, worthy men. I write this to you, hoping you will cherish it, value it, and challenge any obstacle you will face. I am with you. I will never leave you. You are the reason I am breathing.

Symbolic Past, Embracing Love

My two boys are my life. I'll hold you high, and you're my greatest and most special prize. I wouldn't truly be your mother if my story was hidden under covers. I would like to say sorry. Sorry for the generation you were brought up in. I'm sorry that respect is now just among friends. Sorry for the days that I couldn't give you what you needed. I know sometimes I took my anger out on you, and I know that's not right. I am sorry for the nights when you questioned if I loved you.

My first, I am sorry your dad wasn't man enough to be your dad. I feel I failed you, and I cry sometimes, but it's weird, because your dad's absence makes me glad. I'll let you question him when you're older. I'll prepare you, in case he gives you the cold shoulder. I was young and stupid. I was looking for love. I believed that he loved me and cherished me; but instead, he gave you a sibling after he cheated on me. I raised you for a bit in a shelter. That place changed my life. Never grow up and take things for granted. Always give your hand, sometimes even stretch it. When you have your children, always ask for their mother's hand in marriage. Give your children stability. I am sorry if you feel that that wasn't me. You were born into something that you never asked for. The hardest feeling is when your heart feels poor. Respect will get you far, so never disrespect an elder; they can tell you what kind of man you are. One of the biggest things that I have to say sorry for is if I ever made you feel as though I loved your brother more than I loved you. You are my firstborn, my green-eyed bandit, and much more. If I could go back and change one thing, it would be my life and the way I handled certain things. I'm still struggling to find the meaning. You are the reason I got out of the street life. I wasn't going to tell you at all. I was afraid you would judge me. I am so scared of the upcoming generation. I would never want you to become the old me. Never let your friends tell you where you stand in life. Never let them be the ones to put something in your hand, like a gun or a knife. If you ever feel lost or out of place, you need to pray to the highest place. Ask God to bring you closer to him. Without him, you will always look in the mirror and doubt him. Never let the devil win. He will drag you down. He, too, was once an angel, but he was thrown out of Heaven for his pride. Always know that you can come and talk to me. I'll never lie to you; you can trust me. Never be led astray. The strongest man gets on his knees and prays. Real men shed tears; never let your pride control your fears. Knowledge is more than important, it helps you grasp and understand the ones that are potent. Think and look outside the box. Never let anyone make you conform to how they think our culture looks. Your neighbour may be white, Black, or Chinese, but always remember to greet them how you greet me. Don't let the media make you believe hate. They keep portraying it. They're the ones that help the government. Everyone's just trying to get paid. I love you, my son. Please forgive me, but I can't say that I am truly a woman if I can't show you my true face.

My light-skinned baby, my second born, you are truly a blessing. Sometimes I think that I still didn't learn my lesson. I tried to give you and your brother a family, but your dad needed to marry me. He wasn't really around when you were first born. We were going through a lot of problems, and we were looking to the wrong people while trying to solve them. Two wrongs don't make a right. You were born in December. I'm going to tell you the truth about someone whom you could call your twin brother. It was back in 2010, and I got pregnant. I was happy, but the instability and insecurity scared both your father and me. Your dad asked me to have an abortion. I looked at him like the devil, and I couldn't trust him. He told me he wanted me to succeed, and having a baby right then wasn't a need. I blamed him for a very long time. There's still a day that I cry. I was four-and-a-half months pregnant when the procedure took place. I had to put on a brave face. There was a lady there, and it was as if she could read my spirit. I knew in my heart that I didn't want to do it. Since I was far along, we buried him. The name we gave him was the same as yours, that's why I call him your twin. He's your brother, but he's watching you from the stars. October 5, 2010 was the day he was buried. Every time I go past that intersection, my heart cringes. It's hard to go back to the cemetery. I want you to learn from this. I need you to build before settling down and having a baby. You never know what emotional damage an abortion has. I am not a murderer. There are days when I have to keep telling myself that. I look at you and your brother, and I wonder where he would fit. An abortion is degrading. They just place you on a table, write down a number, then tell you it's time to change places. They tell you to make sure you're not emotional, because that just makes it longer. Every day I regret that I didn't bear your brother. You are a gem in my life, my son. I am not afraid, because I know exactly how to deal with my pain. Make sure you treat your woman right. You came from a woman, so never feel as though you can disrespect one. Social media is bad. If you have a weak mind, your values will begin to erode. Broken families are what is portrayed, and usually it's a black child that they use to throw shade. A lot of us are still together. I can say your father and I are one of them. We both came from broken families, so we both know the importance of stability. My promise to you is that I'll try and be the best mother I can. I can show you the way and the path, but it is up to you to take heed to what I am saying. Never settle for less. You're my strength, my heart, and a come-up from my past. I thank God for you, and I am lucky and blessed that God gave me you, too. You are more than just my son. You are a gift that I can look at and say I proudly won. This isn't a letter, just a symbol of my love, and a reminder of where you came from. I want you to understand that our family unit will always, and should always, be number one.

Diary, I can't stop crying. That was the hardest thing I ever had to write. My children are my life. They are the reason I have become the woman I am today. I am struggling to come to terms with something with one of my children, but I know you won't tell anybody. So how come I am still scared to write it? Maybe because I know there is a possibility of someone else seeing it, but I have to take a stand for myself and my kids, to let them know to be proud of themselves, regardless of what labels they might receive and the hurdles they have to jump. My oldest son, he is honestly a good kid, and he is very smart. He is recognized as gifted by a lot of people. However, I've noticed certain things from when he started junior kindergarten, besides having to pay seven dollars for an agenda. I am sorry, but I had to throw that part in there,

Diary. Shortly after he started school—he is in grade five now—it was time for me to take action for him. I got tired of phone calls from the school, saying he had a bad day. It just kept getting worse, to the point where I began to see that he was being easily influenced by his peers. One day I got a phone call that he was missing around 4:10 pm that day. I was just leaving work, and the way my heart felt, I could swear it wasn't even beating. I struggled to breathe. All I could do was drive, and drive as fast as I could to the daycare.

I was so upset, because school had ended an hour ago, and someone was just calling me now. Some older kids at his school had dared him to go to the store down the street after school had ended. At that point, I realized it had gone too far, and I needed to do something immediately to save him, before he became a product of his environment and a stereotypical Black child. I brought him to our family doctor to talk about why he got so angry so fast. The doctor referred us to a psychiatrist to get an assessment. Sigh, this is still hard for me to accept. He was diagnosed with ADHD and anxiety disorder. I am still struggling with the diagnosis. I kept it to myself for awhile before telling my family. Some cultures don't recognize mental health, and believe that the child just needs the correct discipline, which I believe is a part of it, but it is not all of it. Times have changed, food has changed, and the processing has changed. I was very apprehensive about putting my child on medication, because as a worker in this field, I see that some children lose their personality. I shared my concerns with the psychiatrist, and she started him on a low dosage of 18mg to start.

CHANGE

I have noticed a slight difference at school, Diary. He is able to earn more incentives, and he doesn't challenge his teachers as much. But now it's time to get some professional help, like counselling. I know that my son is going through a lot. I know he is struggling with rejection from his biological dad. His dad attempted to come back around in October of 2016. I brought him to see him. I was so upset while I was there, but I tried my hardest not to show it. His dad was obviously nervous to see him after seven years, but I was upset at the fact that he never really spent time with him. It was as if he was trying to avoid the situation. He gave him money, and my son then thought he was the greatest dad ever, and couldn't wait to go back to see him. His father and I kept in contact for just a few days more after that.

I spoke to him about our son seeing him again, and he wanted me to bring him over to his house, again. I declined that request and tried to explain to him that he needed to put in the effort and come and see his son. And when I brought him, all he was doing was playing dominoes at his neighbour's house, instead of spending time with his son or getting to know him. I felt as if I had wasted my time. He responded by saying that he wasn't going to let anybody tell him how to live his life, and if that was the case, then he would wait until he got older. I cried myself to sleep that night, and I blamed myself for even bringing him to see his dad. But it had been so long that I thought maybe he had actually changed and grown up. I now had to explain to my son that he wasn't going to be around, and explain to him why, in a way that he could understand.

The night came that I decided to tell him, and he completely shut down, Diary. He shut down and destroyed his room that night. I felt so bad. He cried, and I cried. I tried to reassure him that everything was going to be okay. I called my fiancé and told him what was going on, and I greatly appreciated that he said that he was going to step up in the role that he played in my son's life, and he would have a talk with him to let him know what a father is and that he was there for him. The next morning, he appeared to be in good spirits. He never brought up his dad at all. He gave me a hug and said he loved me. I tried to talk to him before he went to school, but he didn't respond. He told me that he didn't want to go to school. When I got to the daycare to drop him and his brother off, I told him that I would run inside to drop off his brother, and then he and I could talk before he went inside for school. That would give me some alone time with him so that he could express himself and talk without his little brother interrupting our conversation.

Diary, brace yourself for what I am about to tell you. I cry as I write this to you. My heart still bleeds from this. When I got back into the car, my son was trying to kill himself. He had the front passenger seatbelt around the front passenger seat headrest and his neck. I didn't yell at him. I just helped him get free from the seatbelt, and gave him a big hug. He began crying and weeping, "Why doesn't he love me? Why am I not good enough for him?" I didn't know what to do. I just held him for a bit. He said he still wanted to go to school to see his friends. I didn't want to let him go, but to be honest, that's how I deal with my pain, too.

I just tried to keep myself busy that day. After I dropped him off, I cried the entire way to work. I cried at work. I called my son's school, crying. I was a hot mess that day, and to be honest, I wanted to go to his dad's house and fight him, but I knew that wasn't going to solve anything. I spoke to my son's teacher, and then I spoke to his school social worker, just so that they would keep an eye out for him. The social worker said she was going to see him immediately, to touch base with him. I didn't know how much more I could honestly take. Diary, I felt as if my life was going on a downward spiral, and I didn't know what to do. I have a pretty good handle on things when it's myself. I know how to deal with my shit; I'm an adult. But my son…that's my child! Why the fuck don't I know what to do? Diary, just answer me this one time, please. That's all I ask. I tell you all my secrets. Please, just answer me this one fucking time. I don't ask you for anything but to just listen to me. Haven't you heard enough? Don't you have anything to say to me?

I can't do this by myself anymore. I need help. I need help, and I need it now. I needed to tell my family about my son, so I could get their support. I just needed something or someone to help, please. I took a picture of the letter that the psychiatrist wrote for the school with recommendations to help further his success at school, and I sent it to my brother, mom, and dad. I knew my mom would have a lot to say to challenge it. She immediately thought that they were labelling my son. I didn't even debate with her on it. I just left it, because I knew in my heart there was nothing to debate anymore. I had made up my mind—I chose to accept it and do something about it. When I told my brother, we ended up having a nice conversation about it. His first response to me was along the lines of, "Is there something wrong with that? Because I don't see a problem."

I was taken aback by his response, but it reminded me of why he and I are so close, and the man and father he had become. He sent me some videos of experts talking about the development of children. I watched them, and they were quite empowering. My brother also encouraged me to come over more, and to remind my kids every day that I love them, no matter what challenges each day brings. I told my dad, and to be honest, I thought he was going to be totally against the diagnosis. I could tell he was, Diary, but he didn't challenge me at all. He just said, "Okay," and asked what I was going to do about it. I didn't tell them about the medication piece. I just wasn't ready to tell them about that, because I didn't want to have a battle with my family over the choices that I made for my children. I also called an agency that would go and observe him with his peers, and then talk to me afterwards and discuss supports and how to help him.

One thing I can say is that being a Child and Youth Worker, you get to learn the system and the processes you have to undertake as a parent and educator to help the children that you serve. I still stress a lot about it every morning when I give him his medication. Diary, I feel as if I just took a breath of fresh air, because that was a heavy load that I needed to get off my chest. Thank you for being there for me. If I am going to tell other people to accept help, I first have to come to terms with anything that I may be facing, emotionally, mentally, and physically. I can't believe that I have been with my partner for eight-and-a-half years, and I love him dearly. He is an amazing person and friend. However, I don't feel in my heart anymore that he is right for me. He doesn't know how to be a man in a relationship, but he is an amazing friend. I had to repeat myself on that one. Everyone has been telling me to leave him, but it is different when you hear everyone in your head telling you to leave someone. Your instinct is to defend your relationship with that person. I had to reach the end by myself, without anybody else telling me what to do. We got into an argument about his inconsistency and not putting our family first. I then went to my son's room and slept in his bed. That was when I realized that I was done and had had enough. But, Diary, my heart and mind were fighting themselves. I know everyone won't believe that I have decided to leave him, so I haven't told a lot of people.

LONGEVITY

⊰⊱

I only told people that I knew would support me one hundred percent, without bias. It was so hard, because why is it that when someone decides to leave, that's when the other person decides to step up to the plate. It had my mind fighting my heart, and I knew it would just be the same routine with him and me. And I knew we were both equally tired of it. I was tired of not being his queen while I placed him as my king. I realized where I went wrong in our relationship: I made him my husband before he made me his wife. My pride was what kept me there so long. I honestly wanted him to be happy, and I needed and wanted to be happy as well. I was no longer happy with our relationship and what it had become. All we did was argue, then have sex, talk every day for about two weeks, and then something would pop up, and then it would go back to being the same thing. I needed more than that out of my relationship and life. He also deserved the same thing. The thing that was really hurting my heart was that I decided to leave days before our seventh year anniversary, and it put a lot of stress and pain on my mind and heart, but I had to do what was right for myself.

The entire situation increased my symptoms of anxiety and panic attacks. I contacted my doctor to get referred to a really good program at a hospital located in the Downtown Toronto area. I am just waiting to hear back from the hospital to start the process of counselling. My thoughts, heart, and mind are all over the place, Diary. I really need to go and buy a new diary to write my thoughts on culturalism and mental health, because I know I need help, Diary. I am sorry I am about to go on a rant, so please prepare yourself. I am tired of people saying that everything will be okay. No, everything will not be okay, unless you choose to do something about it to fix your situation, and not a lot of people know how to do it or where to start. I know I am having a panic attack right now just thinking of all the shit I have been through and haven't dealt with until now. The first sign that I am having a panic attack is that my head starts to feel light, and then I feel as if I have to move my head very fast in a circle and move my body very fast, or else my body will shut down. It's absolutely crazy, and it's getting more intense as each month passes by.

It has gotten to the point where smells and places trigger it. I don't know if it's my subconscious mind that remembers certain things with certain smells, but it's scary, and not a good feeling. This shit happens when I am out with family and even friends. I don't go out a lot, and all my friends comment on that, and call me a granny. But the truth is that I don't go out often so that I don't have to have a panic attack while out with them, because the smallest thing can bring on a panic attack for me. I have never told my friends that I am suffering from this. People don't understand that everyone is different, and everyone deals with everything differently. Diary, before I got you, there was a lot of shit that I went through. I thank God that you were given to me, and I am upset that it took me a long time to finally use you on a consistent basis. Dealing with my parents separating; my uncle molesting me for years; having to go to family events, knowing he was there; finding out about my biological mom; being in foster care; dealing with my parents' new significant others; feeling like my dad loved my brother more than me; going to jail several times over the years; having an abortion; burying my child; getting into drugs and violence; faking pregnancies to keep safe in the streets, because when beef got real, it was real; losing several friends to gun violence each year; having my son's father abandon me and his child; living in a shelter; being on probation; being taken from one parent and then going to live with another parent outside of town; having my biological mom tell me that being molested is a part of life; not knowing who my real biological father is, because my mom lied to me about who he really was; having my dad drop me off at my aunt's house and not come back for me; having an eight-and-a-half year relationship that had lots of ups and downs, emotional abuse, physical abuse, domestic violence, and everyone telling me to leave the person I loved; having social services involved in my family and business.

WHAT I DON'T UNDERSTAND IS THAT PEOPLE STILL TELL ME THAT IT IS ALL GOING TO BE OKAY, AND IT WON'T. MENTAL HEALTH IS VERY REAL, AND I CAN'T WAIT TO CONTINUE TO EDUCATE OTHERS ABOUT MENTAL HEALTH AND LIVING WITH MENTAL HEALTH.

Diary, you have been such a great listener, and I thank God that my mom gave you to me. I remember picking you up and reading the first couple of pages about my uncle, and that just inspired me to keep going and to write my story. Diary, you're on your last page now, but I need help with something. Remember how I told you about my son's real-dad situation? It's just sticking to my mind. Here is what happened and how we got in contact. I know you can't answer, but just read and think of what I can do. I plan on just going quiet for awhile, but I just wanted you to know where things are before I continue my story. I was on the phone with my friend, and I saw that my older son's dad's mom was calling, so I told my friend to go on mute. But it wasn't his mom; it was actually him. He thought that I was his cousin at first, but then he quickly realized who he was really talking to. We actually had a good conversation. He said that he wanted to see his son. I spoke to him about him being serious, and not being in and out of his life. He understood where I was coming from. When I got off the phone with him, my friend said I should go and take my son to meet him.

I spoke to my fiancé about it, and he said that I should take him. That's why this shit hurts so much, Diary. I already knew he wasn't being genuine. Diary, I even gave him our son's schedule for MMA class. To see my son hurting, Diary, is something that I want to take away. But the sad part is that I can't take his pain away. Unfortunately, this is the life that a lot of children have to face, and at an early age. Something needs to change.

We need more mentors for our brothers, fathers, and sons. I had that guilty feeling again, that I had failed my son, and I just didn't know what to do to make things right. The fact of the matter is, this isn't something that I can make right. This is just something I can support my son with, while he goes through it.

I just don't know how much strength I have left inside of me, Diary. I am going to get another diary, because I am now down to the last few lines. So thank you for everything, and thank you for still loving me after all of this. It's a shame that so many people feel that living in the dark is what is best to keep them safe from the outside world, but it's not. You have taught me that the voice starts within, and that nobody can tell you when the time is right. You have to get there on your own, and in your own way. I love you so much, Diary, and I promise you that I will continue my story to help those who are struggling with mental health, and even the acceptance of mental health. Just remember, I won't ever forget you on my journey. It all started with you. Thank you!

P.S. I am going to stick a letter on your back, so you know that my story continues. I bought another diary, but I feel that you should know this new, amazing information before the new one does. I love you, Diary! You hold a sentimental place in my heart. xoxoxo

My Sweetest Rose

You came at the beginning of the month of May in 2019. I went through it with you on my own. You were my best friend from the beginning. Our bond was unbreakable the moment I laid my eyes on you, my daughter, my princess. The day my cousin was laid to rest was the day God gave me you to lie upon my chest. That's the day you were conceived. I knew you were going to be a girl. Your father and I planned you. We wanted to show you our love was true, and all the beautiful things even in this corrupt world. We gave you a brother before you. He absolutely loves you, and your other older brother loves you, too. Your dad and I decided to officially part ways when I was about three months pregnant with you. We realized our relationship was stagnant, especially with the bullshit with other females. Your beautiful light-brown eyes and your little thick thighs, you were beyond my strength. You opened my eyes in all the right ways. You, my baby girl, gave me new love in the realest way. My partner in crime, you brought back my life with shine. I felt like giving up in every way. When I pushed you out, I was by myself, but when I saw your face, I felt real wealth. Your purity and beauty instantly healed my emotions. You were the one that made me make a plan and profit. I deserved real love. I wasn't anybody's puppet. I broke my silence and evolved. I am a woman, your mom, and I vow to make you and your brothers proud. Your name is very powerful to me, my little princess, my heart used to bleed. I was lost in the streets. Your name came from a movie about a girl who reminded me of me. You are going to be the better version of me, a true queen. Never make someone belittle you to your knees. Stand up with intellect, and even the ones that don't like you will have to show you the basic respect. You're going to be a beautiful Black woman. Hold your head high. Society will try to break you. I will instil values in you that will guide and protect you. You'll always be my little girl, but more importantly, my brightest angel!

"The highest human act is to inspire." ~Nipsey Hussle

www.ingramcontent.com/pod-product-compliance
Lightning Source LLC
Chambersburg PA
CBHW030906080526
44589CB00010B/171